Calin Rotaru

Color Image Processing for Advanced Driver Assistance Systems

Calin Rotaru

Color Image Processing for Advanced Driver Assistance Systems

Dissertation

Südwestdeutscher Verlag für Hochschulschriften

Impressum/Imprint (nur für Deutschland/ only for Germany)
Bibliografische Information der Deutschen Nationalbibliothek: Die Deutsche Nationalbibliothek
verzeichnet diese Publikation in der Deutschen Nationalbibliografie; detaillierte bibliografische
Daten sind im Internet über http://dnb.d-nb.de abrufbar.
Alle in diesem Buch genannten Marken und Produktnamen unterliegen warenzeichen-, marken-
oder patentrechtlichem Schutz bzw. sind Warenzeichen oder eingetragene Warenzeichen der
jeweiligen Inhaber. Die Wiedergabe von Marken, Produktnamen, Gebrauchsnamen,
Handelsnamen, Warenbezeichnungen u.s.w. in diesem Werk berechtigt auch ohne besondere
Kennzeichnung nicht zu der Annahme, dass solche Namen im Sinne der Warenzeichen- und
Markenschutzgesetzgebung als frei zu betrachten wären und daher von jedermann benutzt
werden dürften.

Verlag: Südwestdeutscher Verlag für Hochschulschriften Aktiengesellschaft & Co. KG
Dudweiler Landstr. 99, 66123 Saarbrücken, Deutschland
Telefon +49 681 37 20 271-1, Telefax +49 681 37 20 271-0, Email: info@svh-verlag.de
Zugl.: Hamburg, Universität Hamburg, Diss., 2008

Herstellung in Deutschland:
Schaltungsdienst Lange o.H.G., Berlin
Books on Demand GmbH, Norderstedt
Reha GmbH, Saarbrücken
Amazon Distribution GmbH, Leipzig
ISBN: 978-3-8381-0714-1

Imprint (only for USA, GB)
Bibliographic information published by the Deutsche Nationalbibliothek: The Deutsche
Nationalbibliothek lists this publication in the Deutsche Nationalbibliografie; detailed
bibliographic data are available in the Internet at http://dnb.d-nb.de.
Any brand names and product names mentioned in this book are subject to trademark, brand or
patent protection and are trademarks or registered trademarks of their respective holders. The
use of brand names, product names, common names, trade names, product descriptions etc.
even without a particular marking in this works is in no way to be construed to mean that such
names may be regarded as unrestricted in respect of trademark and brand protection legislation
and could thus be used by anyone.

Publisher:
Südwestdeutscher Verlag für Hochschulschriften Aktiengesellschaft & Co. KG
Dudweiler Landstr. 99, 66123 Saarbrücken, Germany
Phone +49 681 37 20 271-1, Fax +49 681 37 20 271-0, Email: info@svh-verlag.de

Copyright © 2009 by the author and Südwestdeutscher Verlag für Hochschulschriften
Aktiengesellschaft & Co. KG and licensors
All rights reserved. Saarbrücken 2009

Printed in the U.S.A.
Printed in the U.K. by (see last page)
ISBN: 978-3-8381-0714-1

The cooperation between the Department of Computer Science, University of Hamburg and Group Research Electronics, Volkswagen AG put the basis for this thesis. It is the result of my work in the Driver Assistance Electronics Team during the internship funded by Volkswagen AG. This work was supervised by Prof. Dr. Zhang from the University of Hamburg, Dr. Thorsten Graf and Dr. Rolf Schmidt from the Group Research, Volkswagen AG. I would like first to express my gratitude to them, who knew how to guide, support and show me how to focus my efforts to make this thesis true.

Furthermore, I am also grateful to all other members of the Group Research Electronics Team that helped me during these years. I would like to specially thank in alphabetic order to:

Dr. Alexander Kirchner, Dr. Holger Philipps, Dr. Dirk Stücker and Kristian Weiss that helped me along with the integration of my work into the Sensorfusion system,

Klaus-Dieter Kowalewicz and his team for the work performed to deploy the system into the test vehicle,

Dr. Marian-Andrzej Obojski for his constant assistance during the years,

Jean Schipritt for his excellent work that became part of the object detection and tracking system,

Dr. Will Specks for his kindness and support.

Furthermore, I wish to thank to Andreea Arambasa who have carefully read and corrected this thesis, making it more comprehensible.

And last, but not the least I would like to thank my family and my friends, especially my wife Florentina. Without their friendship, love and support this work would not be what it is.

Contents

1 Introduction   **7**
    1.1 Motivation 7
    1.2 Contribution 8
    1.3 Outline 9
        1.3.1 Environment & Applicability of the solution 9
        1.3.2 Structure 9

2 State of Art   **11**
    2.1 Perception and Computer Vision - Short History 11
    2.2 Vision in Automotive Applications 12
    2.3 Lane Detection 14
        2.3.1 Segmentation-based Approaches 15
        2.3.2 Feature-driven Approaches 16
        2.3.3 Model-driven Approaches 18
    2.4 Object Detection 21
        2.4.1 Image Thresholding 23
        2.4.2 Edge-based methods 23
        2.4.3 Space signature 24
        2.4.4 Background substraction 25
        2.4.5 Inter-frame differencing 25
        2.4.6 Time signature 26
        2.4.7 Feature aggregation and object tracking 26
        2.4.8 Optical flow 27
        2.4.9 Motion parallax 29
        2.4.10 Stereo vision 30
        2.4.11 Inverse perspective mapping 31
        2.4.12 3D modelling and forward mapping 31
    2.5 Color Vision - Short Overview 33
        2.5.1 Mapping the Spectrum onto Perceptual Color Space 33
        2.5.2 Color Spaces used in Computer Vision 34
        2.5.3 Active Research in Color Vision for Active Driver Assistance Systems 35

Contents

3 Image Segmentation in HSI, Lane and Object Recognition — **39**
- 3.1 Generics — 39
  - 3.1.1 Motivation — 39
- 3.2 Image Segmentation Based on SI Metrics — 40
  - 3.2.1 HSI Space Characteristics — 40
  - 3.2.2 Projection of Road Scenes in HSI Space — 42
  - 3.2.3 SI Metrics — 48
  - 3.2.4 Effects of HSI Space Irregularities — 49
  - 3.2.5 Projections of Typical Traffic Scenes on the SI Plane — 51
  - 3.2.6 Adaptive SI Metric Coefficients — 55
  - 3.2.7 Use of the H component — 57
  - 3.2.8 Performance in various illumination conditions — 57
  - 3.2.9 Comparison with other segmentation algorithms — 62
- 3.3 Top-level View — 67
  - 3.3.1 Thread Layout — 69
- 3.4 Road & Lane Detection — 72
  - 3.4.1 Knowledge given by the Automotive Environment — 72
  - 3.4.2 Road Detection based on Intensity and Saturation — 72
  - 3.4.3 Cognitive Lane Marking Detection based on Intensity and Saturation — 77
  - 3.4.4 Lane Marking Detection based on SI Metrics — 78
  - 3.4.5 Lane Delimiters Detection based on Road Detection Results — 81
  - 3.4.6 Yellow Lane Markings — 83
  - 3.4.7 Merging the results - The Lane Interpreter — 87
- 3.5 Object Detection & Tracking — 92
  - 3.5.1 Multiple Models — 92
  - 3.5.2 Object Detection - System Structure — 95
  - 3.5.3 Object Detection - Using SI Metrics — 95
  - 3.5.4 Object Detection - Using Road Information — 97
  - 3.5.5 Object Detection - Lateral Objects — 98
  - 3.5.6 Object Detection - Distant/Far Objects — 100
  - 3.5.7 Filtering the Candidates — 101
  - 3.5.8 Tracking of Objects - Lateral Objects — 102
  - 3.5.9 Tracking of Objects - New Objects — 102
  - 3.5.10 Tracking of Regular Objects - up to about 70 meters — 105
  - 3.5.11 Tracking of Distant/Far Objects - beyond about 70 meters — 108

4 Reconstructing 3D information — **113**
- 4.1 Motivation — 113
- 4.2 Requirements for the Output of a Vision Sensor for Automotive Applications — 113
- 4.3 Projections of the 3D space in the image plane — 114
- 4.4 Reconstruction of 3D Information — 115
- 4.5 Alternative Calibration Methods — 119
- 4.6 Experimental Results — 119

5	**Results**	**121**
	5.1 System architecture	121
	5.1.1 Software Environment	121
	5.1.2 Hardware Setup	124
	5.2 Results	127
	5.2.1 Hardware Platform	127
	5.2.2 Samples of the CCVS processing	128
	5.2.3 Comparison with other vision systems	132
6	**Conclusion & Future Work**	**139**
	6.1 Conclusion	139
	6.1.1 Advantages over existing systems (color, monochrome)	139
	6.1.2 What's New	140
	6.2 Future development	141
7	**Notations and Definitions**	**143**
8	**Appendix**	**145**
	8.1 Short description of included CD	145
	8.2 Tools used to create this document	146
9	**Bibliography**	**147**
	List of Figures	**157**

Contents

1 Introduction

1.1 Motivation

Nowadays, in the automotive domain, electronics plays a much greater role as before. With respect to driving safety and comfort, active driver assistance systems (ADAS) are becoming increasingly important.

One of the first successful applications in active safety was ABS (anti-lock brake system), shortly followed by ESP (electronic stability program). Both of them are, in Europe at least, at the moment series equipment in most new models.

Cruise control is already becoming standard equipment in the Volkswagen Golf segment. Adaptive Cruise Control (ACC) is already present in vehicles belonging to the luxury segment (like Volkswagen Phaeton or Audi A8) and slowly making its way into the middle class (the New Passat for example). ACC already requires more information than the onboard sensor data, i.e. at least a description of the surrounding environment that has a sufficiently high level of representation to allow for the identification of obstacles in front of the car along with their position and speed information. At the moment radar is the sensor of choice for ACC.

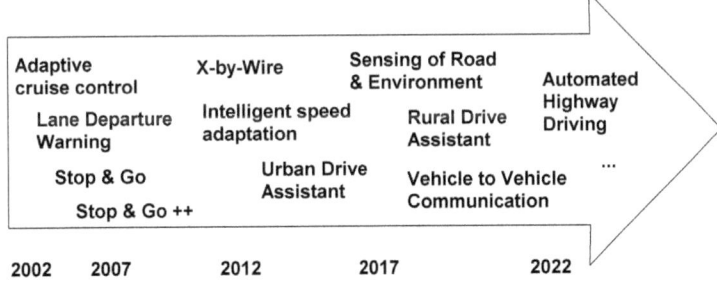

Figure 1.1: The Future of the Driver Assistance Systems

Other driver assistance systems such as Lane Departure Warning are close to becoming series products as can be seen in Fig. 1.1 (courtesy of http://www.foresightvehicle.org.uk). Beside radar or laserscanner information, such advanced systems also require additional input that can only be provided by vision sensors.

7

Chapter 1

The more complex a driver assistance system, the higher the level of representation of the information it requires from sensors. Such a high level representation imposes reliability and safety constraints for the data which can hardly be achieved with a single sensor. Data from multiple sensors has to be merged and interpreted. Such sensors are commonly based on laser, radar, vision or ultrasonic waves. The most complex of them, with regard to the amount of data delivered, is the vision sensor. From the many sensor configurations available for a vision system the most powerful, but still convenient as equipment and deployment costs, is the color mono camera. This thesis focuses on a color mono system built around a consumer electronics camera.

Even if from the hardware point of view the color camera is similar to a gray scale one, from the algorithmic point of view it has a major disadvantage. Usually, a color camera based system has to process 2 to 3 times more data as in the case of a greyscale camera. Therefore until recently, color processing was hardly the subject of online (real time) processing. Not only the lack of hardware resources able to handle the huge amount of data but also the more complex algorithms that are applied on color images caused the processing to be too slow to work online. In the last years advances in the computing architectures made the real time implementation of many algorithms on color data possible. Still the research in the domain remained limited to solving the easiest tasks requiring color information. The great amount of information carried by color data often remained neglected.

As it was often the case in the computer industry, the automotive domain faces nowadays the same dilemma: the hardware costs and availability allow for the use of color cameras, still the software development does not support it. Research in computer vision for the automotive domain has focused mostly on greyscale approaches, with few color specific solutions. This thesis tries to fill in the gap, by describing a color based vision sensor solution targeting the automobile industry.

1.2 Contribution

This thesis adds to the existing research in the field mainly two new approaches to image processing for the automotive domain:

- a realtime approach geared towards making use of the color information to overcome typical difficulties of a greyscale approach. Color information is used to distinguish the vegetation, to detected and follow cars present on the road and to detect their backlights. Indirectly, by using the saturation of the color besides its intensity in almost all segmentation algorithms, an additional sensitivity and robustness is gained.

- a cognitive approach similar to the human perception. Instead of using 3D models projected first on the 2D image plane and afterwards tracked, the approach taken starts with the interpretation of the scene in 2D coordinates or "what could be seen by the video system". This is done without any calibration information, but based on some general assumptions about the environment or "what is expected to be seen by the video system". In the end, this interpretation of the scene is converted back to 3D coordinates required by the applications performing driver assistance functions. In this process some minimal calibration data is required.

1.3 Outline

1.3.1 Environment & Applicability of the solution

The environment targeted in this thesis is the automotive environment, with a special focus on the highway traffic situations. The vision system has to run as a stand alone sensor, being part of a multi-sensorial driver assistance system (Sensorfusion). Its results are to be made available on the industry standard vehicle communication bus, the CAN Bus.

The output of the system has to be used for Automatic Cruise Control on highways in the future after fusion with other sensors. The fusion is performed by the Sensorfusion environment. Therefore the output format of the vision sensor is well defined by the input format for the Sensorfusion.

Minimum requirements for the output are lane and object recognition. Because the Sensorfusion environment is based on the Extended Kalman Filter, the sensor data should ideally not be filtered over time, but the result of a single frame measurement.

1.3.2 Structure

In chapter 2 a review of computer vision, color vision and applications in the automotive domain is presented. The review focuses on past solutions for the lane and object recognition problems addressed in this work.

In chapter 3, after a short introduction, in which the basic requirements are reviewed together with the specifics of the automotive environment, the algorithms used to solve the required tasks are described in detail. These algorithms were developed and programmed during the PhD program. Special attention is paid to the use of color information and to the novel processing techniques.

The conversion of the obtained results from image coordinates to the 3D coordinates follows in chapter 4. Minimal camera calibration requirements are derived together with automatic calibration techniques.

In the beginning of chapter 5, the hardware and software architecture of the system is presented together with details about the integration in the test vehicle. The connection with car systems and the Sensorfusion is shortly presented before the results of the color vision system are compared to other two vision systems that are representative of greyscale processing (stereo and mono). The comparison not only outlines the strengths of the color system, but also reveals the limitations due to the mono camera architecture. It also evaluates the contributions of this work to the already existing research in the field.

The thesis ends with chapter 6, where the conclusions about the advantages resulting from the use of color and novel processing methods are drawn, together with suggestions for future development of the system.

Chapter 1

2 State of Art

2.1 Perception and Computer Vision - Short History

Systematic attempts to understand human vision can be traced back to ancient times.

Euclid (ca. 300 B.C.) wrote about natural perspective. He was well aware of the notion of motion parallax. Although perspective was known to the ancient Greeks, they were curiously confused by the role of the eyes in vision. Aristotle thought that eyes were devices emitting rays (similar to laser range finders). This mistaken view was laid to rest by the work of Arab scientists, such as Alhazen in the 10th century. The mathematical understanding of perspective projection (in the context of projection onto planar surfaces) had its next significant advance in the 15th century in the Italian Renaissance. Brunelleschi, Alberti, da Vinci and Dürer are the best known pioneers in perspective painting.

The development of various kinds of cameras followed. These were rooms ("camera" stands in Latin for chamber) where light entered through a small hole in one wall to cast an image on the opposite wall. Of course, the resulting image was inverted. If such a device was similar to the human eye, how do we see right side up? This enigma exercised the greatest minds of the era, including Leonardo da Vinci. It took the work of Kepler and Descartes to settle the question and find out that the brain is in charge of restoring of the original image.

The next major advances in the understanding of vision took place in the 19th century with the work of Helmholz and Wundt (Handbook of Phsiologial Optics). Through the work of Young, Maxwell and Helmholz, a trichromatic theory of color vision was established. Wheatstone's invention of the stereoscope (1938) brought the idea of stereoscopy (found also in paintings traced back to the late Renaissance in Italy). Eleven years later, Sir Brewer described a binocular camera and put the basis of stereoscopic photography. It will take almost 50 years (1980s) until the correspondence problem was to be completely solved in computer vision and photogrametry.

The period after the World War II was marked by renewed activity. J.J. Gibson (1950, 1979) pointed out the importance of optical flow and texture gradients in the estimation of environment variables such as surface slant and tilt. Gibson, Olum and Rosenblatt (1955) pointed out that the optical flow field contained enough information to determine the egomotion of the observer relative to the environment. Early concerns about the stability of structure from motion were jointly addressed in the work of Tomasi and Kanade (1992). They showed that using multiple frames and the resulting wide baseline, shape could be recovered quite accurately.

A conceptual innovation introduced in the 1990s was the study of projective structure from motion. Faugeras (1992) shown that in this setting the camera calibration was not

Chapter 2

required. This discovery is related to the introduction of the use of geometrical invariants in object recognition, as surveyed by Mundy and Zisserman (1992) and the development of affine structure from motion by Koenderink and Van Doorn (1991). Due to progresses in computer vision hardware and digital video, motion analysis found new applications in 1990s.

Major early works in computer vision about inferring shape from texture are due to Bajscy and Liebermann (1976) and Stevens (1981). Whereas their work targeted planar surfaces, a comprehensive analysis for curved surfaces is due to Garding (1992) and Malik and Rosenholz (1997).

Even earlier shape from shading was approached in computer vision. The first studies can be traced back to Horn (1970). Together with Brooks (1989), he presented an extensive survey of the main papers in the area. Later shape from shading would drive the development of raytracing for the computer graphics.

In the area of interfering shape from contour, after the key initial contributions of Huffman and Clowes (1971), it was Mackworth (1973) and Sugihara (1984) who completed the analysis for polyhedral objects. Malik (1987) developed a labelling scheme for piecewise smooth curved objects.

The seminal work in 3D object recognition was Roberts' (1963) thesis at MIT. It is considered to be the first PhD Thesis in computer vision and it introduced several key ideas like edge detection and model-based matching. Edge detection was later superseded by the work of Canny (1986). Significant improvements in the efficiency of pose estimation by alignment (Lowe, Huttenlocher and Ullman in late 1980s) were obtained by Olson (1994). Another major stand in research on 3D object recognition has been the approach based on the idea of shapes described in terms of volumetric primitives, with generalized cylinders introduced by Binford (1971) ,proving particularly popular.

While object recognition largely focused on issues arising from the projection of 3D objects onto the 2D image plane, there was a parallel tradition in the pattern recognition community that viewed the problem as one of pattern classification. The motivating examples lie in domains such as optical character recognition, handwriting recognition and later face recognition.

In the late 1980s, progresses in the hardware architecture and in the vision hardware had started to make possible the first applications in the automotive domain.

2.2 Vision in Automotive Applications

According to the eSafety Working Group most of the driver assistance systems currently in production or under research focus on the following functions: Antilock Braking System (ABS), **Adaptive Cruise Control (ACC)**, Electronic Stability Program (ESP), Electronic Stability Control for Commercial Vehicles (ESC), **Airbag Electronic Control Unit (ECU)**, **Automatic emergency brake assist (ANB)**, **Lane departure warning system (LDW)**, **Attention control system**, **Traffic signs recognition**, **Automatic distance control (ADC)**, Integral handling control, Assisted or au-

2.2 Vision in Automotive Applications

tomatic parking, **Perceiving vehicle surroundings** or **Enhanced night vision**. The driver assistance functions in bold may profit from using a camera to sense the environment. Some of them need an outside looking vision sensor that delivers lane and object information or validates the results of other sensors. No wonder that the amount of research that was carried out in the field of driver assistance is extremely large. Almost any vehicle supplier has its own research team, major component suppliers as well.

As presented in 2.1, computer vision applications have been around for a few decades already. Still, in the automotive domain, they have only appeared in the last years and most solutions are far from series production. Despite the increasing market demand, the large number of application areas and active research the number of solutions that has been reaching the consumer market has been limited.

This is surprising since the human driving activity relies almost exclusively on visual perception of the infrastructure and of the surrounding traffic. Still, even now, active in-car driver assistance systems like ACC/ADR mostly do not include vision sensors. This is due to cost, performance and reliability issues. Ten years ago video cameras were not a common commodity. This changed with the boom of mobile phones and personal organizers. Microprocessor performance increased exponentially in the same decade. In the last few years the computer industry focuses on creating lower power solutions. Everyday researchers around the world create new or better algorithms and solutions for driver assistance functions. All these suggest that it will not be long before the field of vision applications in the automotive domain will literally skyrocket.

Indeed, few driver assistance systems in series production are already present on the market, and many others have been announced. Lane departure warning, improved ACC solutions by using vision and radar sensors, dead-angle surveillance, park assistance are only a few to name.

The extreme requirements that have to be satisfied in the automotive domain have always limited the number of solutions. Maybe the most difficult requirements are given by the realtime online operation and the non-controlled environment with extreme lightning conditions. Availability and reliability play also a major role in the adoption of a system by the market.

Still, these challenges have not succeeded in discouraging the research in the field, they have only stimulated it. In the last years, the research in image processing in the automotive domain (visible spectrum) has greatly increased as it can be seen from the number of papers that are published annually at two of the most important conferences in the field (see table 2.2).

	2000	2001	2002	2003	2004
IEEE Intelligent Vehicle Symposium	25 (2)	n/a	22 (1)	39 (1)	59 (3)
IEEE Intelligent Transportation Systems Conference	7 (1)	13 (1)	20 (1)	18 (8)	n/a
Intelligent Transportation Systems World Congress	n/a	n/a	n/a	11 (0)	7 (2)

Chapter 2

The numbers in brackets are the number of published papers on the subject of color image processing. This remained constantly low (with a single exception at ITSC 2004). The reason is that the advantages of color processing were considered insignificant in comparison with the difficulties that arise from the processing of almost 3 times more data and using more complicated algorithms. This is slowly changing as technical advances allow complex algorithms to run in real time.

As standalone sensors for automotive applications, vision systems accomplish mainly two tasks: estimation of road geometry (including ego vehicle position) and object (obstacle or infrastructure) recognition. Road or lane recognition deals with the estimation of the lane parameters and the positioning of the ego vehicle in the lane. Object recognition refers to the detection and eventually the identification of various objects on the road (vehicles, pedestrians, etc.), off the road (poles, trees, etc.) or of the traffic signs, traffic lights or other infrastructure elements. The survey in the next sections will focus on lane and obstacle (car) detection since they are the subject of this thesis.

2.3 Lane Detection

The lane detection process in case of driver assistance systems is designed to (i) provide position and orientation of the ego car within the driving lane (ii) provide details about the road structure (current lane size is the most common requirement) and (iii) infer a reference system for locating other vehicles or obstacles in the path of that vehicle. Although some systems have been designed to work on completely unstructured roads and terrain, lane detection has generally been reduced to the localization of specific features, such as lane markings painted on the road surface.

Real-time road segmentation is complicated by the great variability of vehicle and environmental conditions. Weather conditions, dirt on the road, shadows, reflections when the sun is at low angle, and manmade changes (tarmac patches used to repair road segments) pose many challenges both to the hardware and software of the video sensor. Therefore robust segmentation is very demanding. Several features of structured roads, such as color and texture, can be used to distinguish between road and non-road regions in each individual frame. Furthermore, road tracking can facilitate road segmentation based on previous information. This process, however, requires knowledge of the vehicle dynamics, vehicle suspension, performance of the navigation and control systems, etc. Single-frame analysis has been extensively considered not only in monocular but also in stereo vision systems. The approaches used in stereo vision often involve independent processing on the left and right images and projection of the result to the ground plane through the Helmholtz shear equation, making the assumption of flat road and using piecewise road geometry models (such as clothoids) [113], [112]. Furthermore, the inverse perspective mapping can be used to simplify the process of lane as well as object detection [12]. The inverse perspective mapping essentially re-projects the two images onto a common plane (the road plane) and provides a single image with common lane structure. A more general approach is presented in [81] using a generic 3D reconstruction of the vertical edge points and grouping the resulted lane delimiters in order to interpolate the clothoid model of the lane.

In the case of a moving vehicle, the lane recognition process must be repeated continuously on a sequence of frames. In order to accelerate the lane detection process, there is a need to restrict the computation to a reduced region of interest (ROI). There are two possible approaches. The first restricts the search on the predicted path of the vehicle by defining a search region within a trapezoid on the image plane, which is located through the perspective transform. The second approach defines small search windows located at the expected position of the lane, separated by short spatial distances. A rough prediction of the lane position at subsequent video frames can highly accelerate the lane detection process.

Already existing lane recognition systems can be classified into 3 main classes [105]: lane/road region detection, feature driven and model driven.

2.3.1 Segmentation-based Approaches

Segmentation-based approaches try to classify the image pixels into at least road and no-road classes based on particular features. The typical solution involves: (i) feature extraction, (ii) decorrelation and reduction, (iii) clustering and (iv) segmentation.

According to [101] [104] two features are mainly used in the process. For low resolution images the intensity is the feature of choice, while for higher resolution pictures texture can be used as well. In color image processing, the intensity may be replaced by various combinations between R,G,B values. These are used to highlight the specific spectral response of the road surface to light.

In [104] for each pixel the (R,G,B) value defines the feature vector. The classification is performed directly on the (R,G,B) scatter diagram of image . The green band contributes very little in the separation of classes in natural scenes and on the (R,B) plane classification can be performed through a linear discriminant function, since road pixels are well separated from the non-road pixels. The classification process in [104] is based on piece-wise linear discriminant functions, in order to account for varying color conditions on the road (shading, reflexions, etc). In [101] the road segmentation is performed using stochastic pattern recognition approaches. One can define many classes representing road and/or non-road segments. Each class is represented by its mean and variance of the (R,G,B) values. The normal distribution is used to model the extent of the color classes.

In either RBG or HSI/V spaces the apparent color of an object is not consistent. It depends on the illuminant color, the reflectivity of the object, viewing geometry and the sensor type (CMOS, CCD, 3CCD) and its parameters. Thus, color as a feature for classification requires special treatment and normalization to ensure consistency of the classification results. Once the road has been localized in an image, the color statistics of the road and non-road models need to be modified in each class, adapting the process to changing conditions [15]. The Hue, Saturation, Value (HSV) space may sometimes prove more effective for the classification [5].

If the resolution of the acquired image permits it, the local texture of the image is the

Chapter 2

second feature used for the classification [101] [119] besides color/intensity. The texture of the road is normally smoother than that of the environment, allowing for region separation in its feature space. The texture calculation is based on the amplitude of the gradient operator at each image area. In [101] a normalized gradient measure based on a high resolution and a low resolution (smoothed) image is used to handle shadow interior and boundaries. Texture classification can be performed through stochastic pattern recognition techniques and unsupervised clustering. Since the road surface is poorly textured and distinct from objects and background, grey level segmentation has a chance of discriminating the road area from other surfaces. Unsupervised clustering on the basis of C-means algorithm and the Kohonnen self-organizing maps are employed in [49] on a 3D input feature space. Two of the dimensions of the space are given by the position information and the third signifies the greylevel of each pixel under consideration. In order words, the classifier groups together pixels having similar intensities and that are close positioned in the image.

Normally, the classification step outputs a lot of small regions. Their size, depending on the sensitivity of the segmentation, may prove too small for a later interpretation. The classification step must be followed by region merging in order to combine similar small regions under a single label. Region merging may utilize other information, such as motion. A map of static regions obtained by simple frame differencing can provide information about the motion activity of neighbouring patches candidate for merging [49]. Texture classification can also be effectively combined with color classification based on the confidence of the two classification schemes [101].

2.3.2 Feature-driven Approaches

Feature-driven approaches involve two steps [105] (i) feature detection and (ii) feature aggregation. To improve the results, some preprocessing of the image may be done, such as noise suppression or enhancement of the features (for example edges).

More generally the feature detection part aims at extracting discontinuities in the intensity. There are few approaches based on color [88] since the searched features (lane markings) are by definition white elements on a dark background, therefore the major part of their information as image feature will be encoded in the intensity component. The benefits of color become important when dealing with yellow markings [89] or with a green background [94] for non structured environment (all terrain vehicles).

Feature aggregation groups and organizes the detected features (edges for example) into meaningful structures (lane markings) based on short-range or long-range attributes. Short-range aggregation considers local lane fitting into the edge structure of the image. A realistic assumption for all regular drive scenarios, in which the movement of the ego vehicle follows the flow of the lane, is that the position of the lane markings does not change radically from one image to the next in the sequence. Hence the previous detection step will give the position of the search regions for the next image. In a more complex approach [81] the size of the search areas is given from the previous estimations by using the estimation of the measurement error by means of Kalman filtering. In these regions,

2.3 Lane Detection

after the features are detected, they are filtered and clustered. Long-range aggregation is based on a line intersection model, assuming a smooth road curvature. Thus road boundaries and lane markings are converging to a point in the image following the chosen representation of the lane. This point is often called [105] "focus of expansions of the camera system" (FOE).

[58] focuses on the detection of edges in the image and their organization in meaningful structures (lane delimiters). The edge extraction is performed using a gradient operator. The dominant edges are extracted based on the thresholding of the gradient magnitude and refined through thinning operators. At this stage, the direction of edges at each pixel can be computed based on the phase of the gradient and the curvature can be estimated based on neighbourhood relations.

[12] detects lane markings through a linear edge detector. The input image is enhanced using a morphological operator to improve the vertical edges. For each horizontal line, the correspondences of edge points to a two-lane road model (three lane delimiters) are found. The approach identifies the most frequent lane width along the image, through a histogram analysis. All pairs of edge pixels (along each horizontal line) that fall within some limits around this width are considered as lane markings. Corresponding pixels on different scan lines are aggregated together as lines of the road. The Road Markings Analysis (ROMA) system is based on aggregation of the gradient direction at edge pixels in real-time [30]. To detect edges that are possible markings or road boundaries, it employs a contour following algorithm based on the range of acceptable gradient directions. This range is adapted in real-time to the current state variables of the road model. Most of the systems claim to be able to cope with discontinuities in the markings, some being even able to cope with road intersections.

[82] detects brightness discontinuities and retains only long straight lines pointing towards the FOE. For each edge point, the edge direction and the curvature of the neighbouring line are preserved. A first elimination of edges based on thresholding of the direction and curvature is done. This keeps only straight lines pointing towards the specific direction of the FOE. The feature aggregation is performed through correlation with a synthetic image that encodes the road structure for the specific FOE. The edge detection can be efficiently performed through morphological operators [11] [6] [117].

[65] operates on search windows located along the estimated position of the lane markings. For each search window, the edges of the lane marking are determined as the locations of maximum positive and negative horizontal changes in illumination. These edge points are aggregated as boundaries of the lane making (paint stripe) based on their spacing, which should approximate the lane-marking width. The detected lanes at near-range are extrapolated to far-range via linear least squares fit, to provide an estimated lane-marking location for placing the subsequent search windows. The location of the road markings along with the state of the vehicle are used as input to two different Kalman filters that estimate the near and far-range road geometry ahead of the vehicle [65]. Prior knowledge of the road geometry imposes strong constraints on the location and orientation of the lanes.

Alternatively, other features that capture information about the orientation of the

Chapter 2

edges, but are less sensitive to extraneous edges, have been proposed. Along these lines, the LANA algorithm [63] uses frequency-domain features rather than features directly related to the detected edges. These feature vectors are used along with a deformable-template model of the lane markers in a Bayesian estimation setting. The deformable template introduces a priori information, whereas the feature vectors are used to compute the likelihood probability. The parameters of the deformable template are estimated by optimizing the resulting maximum aposteriori objective function [63]. Simpler linear models are used in [5] for road boundaries and lane markings, with their parameters estimated via a recursive least squares (RLS) filter fit to candidate edge points.

In general, feature driven approaches are highly dependent on the methods used to extract features and they suffer from noise effects and irrelevant feature structures. In practice, the strongest edges do not correspond to road edges, so that the detected edges do not necessarily fit a straight-line or a smoothly varying model. Edges due to shadows, vehicles or road imperfections can appear quite strong, highly affecting the line tracking approach. To cope with these problems, the systems rely heavily on restricting the search regions by using a standard lane width and/or tracking the results.

2.3.3 Model-driven Approaches

Model-driven approaches differ categorically between stereo and mono vision. While stereo vision can use its 3D reconstruction capability to match a 3D model derived from the image with the road model, mono vision to start with some assumptions about the road (like flat road, simpler models with limited curvatures, small pitch angles, etc).

Model-driven approaches match a mathematical model defining the road lane to the acquired image features. The parameters of the mathematical model are derived and tracked. Road edges and lane markings are often approximated by circular arcs on a flat-ground plane. More flexible approaches have been considered in [118] [111] using snakes and splines to model road segments. In contrast to other deformable line models, [111] uses a spline-based model that describes the perspective effect of parallel lines, considering simultaneously both-side borders of the road lane. For small to moderate curvatures, a circular arc is approximated by a second-order parabola, whose parameters must be estimated. The estimation can be performed on the image plane [59] or on the ground plane [111] by empoying first an inverse perspective mapping. Bayesian optimization procedures are often used for the estimation of these parameters.

Model-based approaches for lane detection have been extensively employed in stereo vision systems, where the estimation of the 3D structure is possible. Such approaches assume a parametric model of the lane geometry. A tracking algorithm estimates the parameters of this model from feature measurements in the left and right images [82]. In [97] the lane tracker predicts where the lane markers should appear in the current image based on its previous estimates of the lane position. It then extracts possible lane markers from the left and right images. These feature measurements are passed to a robust estimation procedure, which recovers the parameters of the lane along with the orientation and height of the stereo rig with respect to the ground plane. The Helmholtz

2.3 Lane Detection

shear equation is used to verify that candidate lane markers actually lie on the ground plane [97]. The lane markers are modeled as white bars of a particular width against a darker background. Regions in the image that satisfy this intensity profile can be identified through a template matching procedure. In this form, due to the perspective effect, the width of the lane markers in the image changes linearly as a function of the distance from the camera, or the location of the image row considered. Thus, different templates are used at different image locations along the length of the road, in both the left and right images. Once a set of candidate lane markers has been recovered, the lane tracker applies a robust fitting procedure using the Hough transform, to find the set of model parameters which best match the observed data [97]. A robust fitting strategy is absolutely essential in traffic applications, because on real highway traffic scenes the feature extraction procedure almost always returns a number of extraneous features that are not part of the lane structure. These extra features can come from a variety of sources like vehicles on the highway, shadows or cracks in the roadway etc.

Another class of model-driven approaches involves the stochastic modelling of lane parameters and the use of Bayesian inference to match a road model to the observed scene. The position and configuration of the road, for instance, can be considered as variables to be inferred from the observation and the a posteriori probability conditioned on this observation [118] [36]. This requires the description of the road using small segments and the derivation of probability distributions for the relative positions of these segments on regular road scenes (prior distribution on road geometry). Moreover, it requires the specification of probability distributions for observed segments, obtained using an edge detector on the observed image, conditioned on the possible positions of the road segments (a posteriori distribution of segments). Such distributions can be derived from test data [36].

The 3D model of the road can also be used by modelling the road parameters as differential equations that relate motion with spatial changes. Such approaches using state variable estimation (Kalman filtering) are developed in [20] [22]. The road model consists of skeletal lines pieced together from clothoids (i.e. arcs with constant curvature change over their run length). The road assumptions define a general highway scene, where the ground plane is flat, the road boundaries are parallel with constant width, the horizontal road curvature changes slowly (almost linearly) and the vertical curvature is insignificant. Assuming slow speed changes, or piecewise constant speed, the temporal change of curvature is linearly related to the speed of the vehicle. Thus, the curvature parameters and their association with the ego-motion of the camera can be formulated into a compact system of differential equations, providing a dynamic model for these parameters. The location of the road boundaries in the image is determined by three state variables: the vehicle lateral offset from the lane center, the yaw angle of the vision system in the road coordinate system and the horizontal road curvature. A Kalman based filtering algorithm is employed in [74] to estimate the state-variables of the road and reconstruct the 3D location of the road boundaries.

The previous model assumes no vertical curvature and no vertical deviation of the camera with respect to the road. These assumptions imply a flat-road geometry model,

Chapter 2

which is of limited use in practice. Other rigorous models, such as the hill-and-dale and the zero-bank models have been considered for road geometry reconstruction [104] [76]. The hill-and-dale model uses a flat-road model for the two roadway points closest to the vehicle in the image, and forces the road model to move up or down from the flat-road plane so as to retain a constant road width. The zero-bank assumption models the road as a space ribbon generated by a central line-spine and horizontal line-segments of constant width cutting the spine at their midpoint at a normal to the spines 3D direction. Even more unstructured road geometry is studied in [23], where all local road parameters are involved in the state-variable estimation process.

Model-driven approaches provide powerful means for the analysis of road edges and markings. However, the use of a model has certain drawbacks, such as the difficulty in choosing and maintaining an appropriate model for the road structure, the inefficiency in matching complex road structures and the high computational complexity.

The Standard Mathematical Model for the Lane

The most common mathematical representation is based on the clothoid model (third degree equation in the 3D coordinate system). Using a clothoid for both horizontal and vertical curvature allows an accurate representation of all situations encountered in highway scenarios [81]. Country roads are pushing the model to its limits, while intersections require a more complex, piecewise representation (in which for example every road entering the intersection can be modeled by the clothoid model).

A mono camera vision system is limited to the horizontal curvature since it has limited reconstruction abilities (the common assumption is that the road is flat, i.e. no vertical curvature).

In order to describe a lane, the lane width, car position and some other application specific attributes (like marking type, color and so on) must be added to the mathematical model for the clothoid in the 3D space (2.1).

$$X = c_1 * \frac{Z^3}{6} + c_0 * \frac{Z^2}{2} + \tan(-\alpha) * Z + X_0 \qquad (2.1)$$

In (2.1) the coefficients mean: X_0 - position of the ego car in the lane; α - heading angle; Z - the depth at which the horizontal position is computed; c_0 - curvature; c_1 - curvature variation. The equation of the clothoid is presented in (2.1). If the vertical profile is required then to this horizontal description a second clothoid is added to describe the behavior of the road in the vertical plane.

Not all coefficients are used in driver assistance systems. Most of the time some the following parameters are estimated:

- width of the lane
- horizontal curvature and curvature variation
- lateral displacement of the car with respect to the center of the lane (or vice versa)
- angles (yaw -yaw and yaw-rate can also be obtained from car electronics such as ESP-, maybe pitch)

Lane departure warning systems use either the "time to line crossing" (TLC) or the comparison between current angles between the car projection and interpolations of detected lane markings. Both of these values can be computed directly out of the image coordinates [102], respectively [52].

In case of a lane keeping system the most relevant input is the lateral displacement. The heading angle and/or the curvature can be used to stabilize the controller loop or to improve the controller reaction.

The width, lateral displacement and curvature (sometimes also the curvature variation) are used to associate objects detected with other sensors to a certain traffic lane.

2.4 Object Detection

Object detection can be carried out from a stationary camera (e.g. surveillance camera installed on the highway infrastructure), from a mobile camera (installed in the vehicle) or from a mobile aerial camera (satellite, airplane, etc.). Since the research carried out on these topics is very broad, this state of the art will restrict itself to object detection using mobile, in-vehicle camera(s). This is the typical setup for the autonomous vehicle guidance solutions.

Object recognition has been explored by many different research areas in computer vision. Roughly the relevant objects in the automotive applications can be categorized into:
 - passenger cars and trucks
 - bicyclists and motorcyclists
 - pedestrians
 - lateral road delimiters (fences, poles, other infrastructures)
 - road signs and traffic lights
 - other on and off-road obstacles

Such solutions require object detection methods with different abstraction levels. The vision system can facilitate the accurate localization of the vehicle with respect to its environment, by means of matching observations (acquired images) over time, or matching a single observation to a road model or even matching a sequence of observations to a dynamic model.

Two major problems can be identified regarding the efficient recognition of road environment, namely the restricted processing time for real-time applications and the limited amount of information from the environment. For efficient processing the ROI needs to be limited within each frame and process only relevant features within this ROI instead of the entire image. Since the scene in traffic applications does not change drastically, the prediction of the ROI from previously processed frames becomes of paramount importance. Several efficient methods presented in the following are based on dynamic scene prediction using motion and road models. The problem of limited amount of information in each frame stems from the fact that each frame represents a non-invertible projection of the dynamically changing 3D world onto the camera plane. Since single frames encode only partial information, which could be easily misinterpreted, the systems for autonomous vehicle guidance require additional information in the form of a knowledge-

Chapter 2

base that models the 3D environment and its changes (self/ego motion or relative motion of other objects). It is possible from monocular vision to extract certain 3D information from a single 2D-projection image, using visual cues and a priori knowledge about the scene. In such systems, obstacle determination is limited to the localization of vehicles by means of a search for specific patterns, possibly supported by other features such as shape, symmetry, or the use of a bounding box [4], [100], [32]. Essentially, forward projection of 3D models and matching with 2D observations is used to derive the structure and location of obstacles. True 3D modelling, however, is not possible with monocular vision and single frame analysis.

The availability of only partial information in 2D images necessitates the use of robust approaches able to infer a complete scene representation from only partial representations. This problem concerns the matching of a low-abstraction image to a high-abstraction and complexity object. In other words, one must handle differences between the representation of the acquired data and the projected representation of the models to be recognized. A priori knowledge is necessary in order to bridge the gap between these two representations [33]. A first source of additional information is the temporal evolution of the observed image, which enables the tracking of features over time. Furthermore, the joint consideration of a frame sequence provides meaningful constraints of spatial features over time or vice versa. [79] employs smoothness constraints on the motion vectors, which are imposed by the gray-scale spatial distribution. Such form of constraints conveys the realistic assumption that compact objects should preserve smoothly varying displacement vectors. The initial form of integrated spatial-temporal analysis operates on a so-called 2 1 2D feature space, where 2D features are tracked in time. Additional constraints can be imposed through the consideration of 3D models for the construction of the environment (full 3D space reconstruction) and the matching of 2D data (observations) with the 3D representation of these models, or their projection on the camera coordinates (pose estimation problem). Such model information, by itself, enables the consideration and matching of relative object poses [96].

With the latest advances in computer architecture and hardware, it becomes possible to consider even the dynamic modelling of 3D objects. This possibility paved the way for fully integrated spatial-temporal processing, where two general directions have been proposed. The first one considers the dynamic matching of low-abstraction (2D image-level) features between the data and the model. Although it keeps continuous track of changes in the 3D model using both road and motion modelling (features in a 3 1 2D space), it propagates the current 2D representation of the model in accordance with the current state of the camera with respect to the road [60]. Thus, it matches the observations with the expected projection of the world onto the camera system and propagates the error for correcting the current (model) hypothesis [22]. The second approach uses a full 4D model, where objects are treated as 3D motion processes in space and time. Geometric shape descriptors together with generic models for motion form the basis for this integrated (4D or dynamic vision) analysis [21]. Based on this representation one can search for features in the 4D-space [21], or can match observations (possibly from different sensors or information sources) and models at different abstraction levels (or projections) [33].

Some fundamental issues of object detection are considered and reviewed in this section. Approaches have been categorized according to the method used to isolate the object from the background on a single frame or a sequence of frames.

2.4.1 Image Thresholding

Although one of the simplest solutions, thresholding is quite an ineffective technique. It is based on the notion that vehicles are compact objects having different intensity values from their background. Thus, by thresholding intensities in small regions we can separate the vehicle from the background. This approach depends heavily on the threshold used, which must be selected appropriately for a certain vehicle and its background. Simple thresholding techniques are also very sensitive with regard to the acquisition noise. Adaptive thresholding can be used to account for light changes, but cannot avoid the false detection of shadows or missed detection of parts of the vehicle with similar intensities as its environment [86].

To aid the thresholding process, binary mathematical morphology can be used to aggregate close pixels into a unified object [7]. Furthermore, gray-scale morphological operators have been proposed for object detection and identification that are insensitive to lighting variation [115].

A top/down approach is presented in [109]. This method first generates a hierarchy of images at different resolutions. The region search begins at the top level (coarse to fine). Compact objects that differ from their background remain distinguishable in the lowresolution image, whereas noise and small intensity variations tend to disappear at this level. Thus, the lowresolution image can immediately direct attention to the pixels that correspond to such objects in the initial image. The selection of pixels is more complex than simple thresholding, it may be done as a function of the intensity values of its adjacent pixels, edge strength, or successive frame differencing for motion analysis [109].

2.4.2 Edge-based methods

The typical traffic scene contains the image of the rear of the preceding vehicles. These objects are characterized by strong vertical edges and a multitude of both horizontal and vertical edges in the region of backlights. Edge based methods exploit this property. They can be applied to single images to detect the edge structure of even still vehicles [91]. Morphological edge-detection schemes have been extensively applied, since they exhibit superior performance [3] [54] [31].

In traffic scenes, the results of an edge detector generally highlight vehicles as complex groups of edges, whereas road areas yield relatively low edge content. Thus the presence of vehicles may be detected by the edge complexity within the road area, which can be quantified through analysis of the histogram [44].

More complex approaches group the edges together to form boundaries. The used property is the vertical edges are linked by strong horizontal edges. In order to group the edges, they have to be defined as a standalone structure (lines usually) and a grouping strategy must be chosen. Vertical edges are more likely to form dominant line segments corresponding to the vertical boundaries of the profile of a road obstacle. Moreover, a dominant line segment of a vehicle must have other line segments in its neighbourhood that are detected in nearly perpendicular directions. Thus, the detection of vehicles and/or obstacles can simply consist of finding the rectangles that enclose the dominant line segments and their neighbours in the image plane [20]. To improve the shape of object regions [67] [75] employ the Hough transform to extract consistent contour lines and morphological operations to restore small breaks on the detected contours. Symmetry provides an additional useful feature for relating these line segments, since vehicle rears are generally contour and region-symmetric about a vertical central line [64].

Edge-based vehicle detection is often more effective than other background subtraction or thresholding approaches, since the edge information remains significant even in variations of ambient lighting [31].

2.4.3 Space signature

In this detection method, the objects to be identified (vehicles) are described by their characteristics (forms, dimensions, luminosity), which allow identification in their environment [41] [57]. [57] employs a logistic regression approach using characteristics extracted from the vehicle signature, in order to detect the vehicle from its background.

Alternatively, the space signatures are defined in [19] by means of the vehicle outlines projected from a certain number of positions (poses) on the image plane from a certain geometrical vehicle model. A camera model is employed to project the 3D object model onto the camera coordinates at each expected position. Then, the linear edge segments on each observed image are matched to the model by evaluating the presence of attributes of an outline, for each of the pre-established object positions (poses). In a similar framework, [95] projects the 3D model at different poses to sparse 2D arrays, essentially encoding information about the projected edges. These arrays are used for matching with the image data.

Space signatures can also be identified in an image through correlation or template matching techniques, using directly the typical gray-scale signature of vehicles [46]. Due to the inflexible nature of template matching, a specific template must be created for each type of vehicle to be recognized. This creates a problem, since there are many geometrical shapes for vehicles contained in the same vehicle-class. Moreover, the template mask assumes that there is little change in the intensity signature of vehicles. In practice, however, changes in ambient lighting, shadows, occlusion, and severe light reflection on the vehicle body panels generate serious variation in the spatial signatures of same-type vehicles. To overcome such problems, the TRIP II system [19] [108] employs neural networks for recalling space signatures, and exploits their ability to interpolate among different known shapes [71].

Despite its inefficiencies, vehicle detection based on sign patterns does not require high computational effort. Moreover, it enables the system to deal with the tracking process

2.4 Object Detection

and keep the vehicle in track by continuously sensing its sign pattern in real time.

2.4.4 Background substraction

This method is based on forming a precise background image and using it for separating moving objects from their background. The background image is specified either manually, by taking an image without vehicles, or is detected in real-time by forming a mathematical or exponential average of successive images. The detection is then achieved by means of subtracting the reference image from the current image. Thresholding is performed in order to obtain presence/absence information of an object in motion [109] [83] [4].

The background can change significantly with shadows cast by buildings and clouds, or simply due to changes in lighting conditions. With these changing environmental conditions, the background frame is required to be updated regularly. There are several background updating techniques. The most commonly used are averaging and selective updating. In averaging, the background is built gradually by taking the average of the previous background with the current frame. If we form a weighted average between the previous background and the current frame, the background is built through exponential updating [43]. In selective updating, the background is replaced by the current frame only at regions with no motion detected; where the difference between the current and the previous frames is smaller than a threshold [43]. Selective updating can be performed in a more robust averaging form, where the stationary regions of the background are replaced by the average of the current frame and the previous background [31].

2.4.5 Inter-frame differencing

This is the most direct method of making immobile objects disappear and preserving only the traces of objects in motion between two successive frames. The immediate consequence is that stationary or slow-moving objects are not detected. The inter-frame difference succeeds in detecting motion when temporal changes are evident.

However, it fails when the moving objects are not sufficiently textured and preserve uniform regions with the background. To overcome this problem, the inter-frame difference is described using a statistical framework often employing spatial Markov random fields [84] [1] [85]. Alternatively, in [84] the inter-frame difference is modeled trough a two-component mixture density. The two components are zero mean corresponding to the static (background) and changing (moving object) parts of the image. Inter-frame differencing provides a crude but simple tool for estimating moving regions. This process can be complemented with background frame differencing to improve the estimation accuracy [56]. The resulting mask of moving regions can be further refined with color segmentation [25] or accurate motion estimation by means of optical flow estimation and optimization of the displaced frame difference [49] [56], in order to refine the segmentation of moving objects.

Chapter 2

2.4.6 Time signature

This method encodes the intensity profile of a moving vehicle as a function of time. The profile is computed at several positions on the road as the average intensity of pixels within a small window located at each measurement point. The analysis of the time signature recorded on these points is used to derive the presence or absence of vehicles [42]. The time signal of light intensity on each point is analyzed by means of a model with pre-recorded and periodically updated characteristics. Spatial correlation of time signatures allows further reinforcement of detection. In fact, the joint consideration of spatial and time signatures provides valuable information for both object detection and tracking. Through this consideration, the one task can benefit from the results of the other in terms of reducing the overall computational complexity and increasing the robustness of analysis [2]. Along these lines, the adaptable time delay neural network developed for the Urban Traffic Assistant (UTA) system is designed and trained for processing complete image sequences [114]. The network is applied in the detection of general obstacles during the course of the UTA vehicle.

2.4.7 Feature aggregation and object tracking

These techniques can operate on the feature space to either identify an object, or track characteristic points of the object [74]. They are often used in object detection to improve the robustness and reliability of detection and reduce false detection rates. The aggregation step handles features previously detected, in order to find the vehicles themselves or the vehicle queues (in case of congestion). The features are aggregated with respect to the vehicles geometrical characteristics. Therefore, this operation can be interpreted as a pattern recognition task. Two general approaches have been employed for feature aggregation, namely motion-based and model-based approaches [84].

Motion-based approaches group together visual motion consistencies over time [84] [66] [17]. Motion estimation is only performed at distinguishable points, such as corners [66] [53], or along contours of segmented objects [98], or within segmented regions of similar texture [5] [56] [2]. Line segments or points can also be tracked in the 3D space by estimating their 3D displacements via a Kalman filter designed for depth estimation [49] [84] [66] [17]. Model-based approaches match the representations of objects within the image sequence to 3D models or their 2D projections from different directions (poses) [17]. Several model-based approaches have been proposed employing simple 2D region models (mainly rectangles), active contours and polygonal approximations for the contour of the object, 3D models that can be tracked in time and 4D models for full spatial-temporal representation of the object [17] [34].

Following the detection of features, the objects are tracked. Two alternative methods of tracking are employed in [74], namely numeric signature tracking and symbolic tracking. In signature tracking, a set of intensity and geometry-based signature features are extracted for each detected object. These features are correlated in the next frame to update the location of the objects. Next, the signatures are updated to accommodate for changes in range, perspective, and occlusion. In general, features for tracking encode boundary (edge based) or region (object motion, texture or shape) properties of the tracked object. Active contours, such as snakes and geodesic contours are often employed for the description of boundaries and their evolution over the sequence of frames. For region-based features tracking is based on correspondences among the associated target regions at different time instances [84] [38].

In symbolic tracking, objects are independently detected in each frame. A symbolic correspondence is made between the sets of objects detected in a frame pair. A time-sequenced trajectory of each matched object provides a track of the object [74].

2.4.8 Optical flow

Approaches in this class exploit the fact that the appearance of a rigid object changes little during motion, whereas the drastic changes occur at regions where the object moves in and/or out of the background. The optical flow field $u(x,t)$ is computed by mapping the gray-value $g(x - u\delta t, t - \delta t)$ recorded at time $t - \delta t$ at the image point $x - u\delta t$ onto the gray-value g(x, t) recorded at location x at time t: The optical flow field encodes the temporal displacement of observable gray-scale structures within an image sequence. It comprises information not only about the relative displacement of pixels, but also about the spatial structure of the scene. Various approaches have been proposed for the efficient estimation of optical flow field [79] [45] [29] [61]. In general, they can be characterized as (i) gradient-based (ii) correlation based (iii) feature-based and (iv) multigrid methods.

Gradient-based techniques focus on matching $g(x - u\delta t)$ with $g(x,t)$ on a pixel-by-pixel basis through the temporal gradient of the image sequence. In most cases, the intensity variations alone do not provide sufficient information to completely determine both components (magnitude and direction) of the optical flow field $u(x,t)$ [27].

Smoothness constraints facilitate the estimation of optical flow fields even for areas with constant or linearly distributed intensities [45] [29] [61] [80]. Gradient-based techniques yield poor results for poor-texture images and in presence of shocks and vibrations [37]. Under such conditions, correlation-based techniques usually derive more accurate results. Correlation-based techniques search for the maximum shift around each pixel that maximizes the correlation of gray-level patterns between two consecutive frames. Such procedures are quite expensive in terms of computational complexity. Attempts to speed up the computation at the cost of resolution often imply subsampling of the image and computation of the motion field at fewer image points [37].

Feature-based approaches consider the organization (clustering) of pixels into crude object structures in each frame and subsequently compute motion vectors by matching these structures in the sequence of frames. A robust feature-based method for the estimation of optical flow vectors has been developed by Kories and Zimmermann [62]. Each frame is first subjected to a bandpass filter. Blobs representing local maxima and minima of the greylevel are identified as features. The centroids of the detected blobs are tracked through subsequent frames, resulting in optical flow vectors. A related technique is considered in [106], which aims at matching areas of similar intensities in two consecutive frames. To reduce the amount of computation, pixels of interest are segmented prior to matching using background removal, edge detection or inter-frame difference. The accuracy of these techniques is affected by sensor noise (quantization), algorithmic disturbances and, more importantly, perspective distortions and occlusion resulting from typical camera positions. Nevertheless, the methods are suitable for on-line qualitative monitoring, operating at much faster speeds than human operators and without the problem of limited attention spans [106].

Multigrid methods are designed for fast estimation of the relevant motion vectors at low resolution and hierarchical refinement of the motion flow field at higher resolution levels [26]. The multigrid approach in [109] relies upon the organization of similar pixel-intensities into objects, similar to the feature based approaches. This approach, however, identifies object structures at low-resolution levels where it also computes a crude estimate of the motion field from the low-resolution image sequence. The motion vector field is refined hierarchically at higher resolution levels. A related approach is used in the ACTIONS system, where the optical flow vectors are clustered in order to incrementally create candidate moving-objects in the picture domain [27]. For a still camera, moving objects are readily identified by thresholding the optical flow field. The detection of moving objects in image sequences taken from a moving camera becomes much more difficult due to the camera motion. If a camera is translating through a stationary environment, then the directions of all optical-flow vectors intersect at one point in the image plane, the focus of expansion or the epipole [27]. When the car bearing the camera is moving in a stationary environment along a flat road and the camera axis is parallel to the ground, the motion field (due to ego-motion) is expected to have almost quadratic structure [37]. If another moving object becomes visible by the translating camera, the optical flow field resulting from this additional motion will interfere with the optical flow field of the ego-motion. This interference can be detected by testing if the calculated optical-flow vectors have the same direction as the estimated ego-motion model vectors [27] [37]. The detection of obstacles from a moving camera based on the optical flow field is generally divided into two steps. The ego-motion is first computed from the analysis of the optical flow. Then, moving or stationary obstacles are detected by analyzing the difference between the expected and the real velocity fields [28] [66] [16]. These fields are re-projected to the 3D road coordinate system using a model of the road (usually flat straight road) [14] [24].

The estimation of ego-motion can be based on parametric models of the motion field. For planar motion with no parallax (no significant depth variations), at most eight parameters can characterize the motion field. These parameters can be estimated by optimizing an error measure on two subsequent frames using a gradient-based estimation approach [56] [47]. The optimization process is often applied on a multiresolution representation of the frames, to provide robust performance of the algorithm [47]. When the scene is piecewise planar, or is composed of a few distinct portions at different depths, then the ego-motion can be estimated in layers of 2D parametric motion estimation. Each layer estimates motion at a certain depth due to the camera and removes the associated portions of the image. Image regions that cannot be aligned in two frames at any depth are segmented into independently moving objects [47]. For more general motion of the camera, the ego-motion effect can be decomposed into the planar and the parallax parts.

After compensating for the planar 2D motion, the residual parallax displacements in two subsequent frames are primarily due to translational motion of the camera. These displacements due to camera motion form a radial field centred at the epipole. Independently moving objects can be recovered by verifying that the displacement at any given point is directed away from the epipole [48]. The problem of recovering the optical flow from time varying image sequences is ill-posed and additional constraints must be often imposed to derive satisfactory solutions. Smoothness constraints stem from the fact that uniformly moving objects possess slightly changing motion fields. Such constraints have been used in a joint spatiotemporal domain of analysis [77]. [93] first calculates the optical flow and after smoothing the displacement vectors in both the temporal and the spatial domains, it merges regions of relatively uniform optical flow. Finally, it employs a voting process over time in each spatial location regarding the direction of the displacement vectors to derive consistent trends in the evolution of the optical flow field and, thus, define consistently moving objects. In a different form, [70] starts from similarity in the spatial domain. For each frame, it defines characteristic features (such as corners and edges) and matches these features on the present and the previous frame to derive a list of flow vectors. Similar flow vectors are grouped together and compared to the spatial features, in order to verify not only temporal but also spatial consistency of detected moving objects. In a similar form, [70] defines patches of similar spatial characteristics in each frame and uses local voting over the output of a correlation-type motion detector to detect moving objects. It also uses the inverse perspective mapping to eliminate motion effects on the ground plane due to the ego-motion of the camera [70].

2.4.9 Motion parallax

When the camera is moving forward towards an object, the objects projection on the 2D image plane also moves relative to the image coordinate system. If an object extends vertically from the ground plane, its image moves differently from the immediate background. Moreover, the motion of points on the same object appears different relative to the background, depending on the distance from the ground plane. This difference is called motion parallax [16]. If the environment is constrained, e.g. motion on a planar road, then differences observed on the motion-vector can be used to derive information regarding the objects moving within the scene. If we use the displacement field of the road to displace the object, a clear difference between the predicted and the actual position of the object is experienced. In other words, all points in the image that are not on the ground plane will be erroneously predicted. Thus, the prediction error (above an acceptable threshold) indicates locations of vertically extended objects in the scene [16]. If we compensate the ego-motion of the camera, then independently moving (or stationary) obstacles can be readily detected.

The parallax effect is used in a different form for obstacle detection in [103]. A stereo rig is positioned vertically, so that one camera is located above the other. Obstacles

Chapter 2

located above the ground plane appear identical in the camera images, except from their different location. On the other hand, figures on the road appear different on the two cameras. In this configuration, an obstacle generates the same time signature, whereas road figures generate different time signatures on the two cameras. Thus, progressive scanning and delaying one of the camera signals make the detection of obstacles possible. Nevertheless, the system relies on and is highly affected by brightness changes, shadows and shades on the road structure.

2.4.10 Stereo vision

The detection of stationary or moving objects in traffic applications is a typical strength of stereo vision systems. The disparity between points in the two stereo images relates directly to the distance of the actual 3D location from the cameras. For all points lying on a plane, the disparity on the two stereo images is a linear function of image coordinates (Helmholtz shear equation). This Helmholtz shear relation highly simplifies the computation of stereo disparity. It may be used to re-map the right image onto the left, or both images onto the road coordinate system, based on the given model of the road in front of the vehicle (e.g. flat straight road) [68] [113] [97] [4] [18]. All points on the ground plane appear with zero disparities, whereas residual disparities indicate objects lying above the ground plane and can become potential obstacles. A simple threshold can be used to identify these objects in the difference of the re-mapped images.

Besides the projection of images onto the ground plane, stereo vision can be effectively used for the reconstruction of the 3D space ahead of the vehicle. This reconstruction is based on correspondences between points in the left and right images. Once this has been accomplished, the 3D coordinates of the matched point can be computed via a reprojection transform. The approach in the Path project [97] considers such a matching of structural characteristics (vertical edges). Candidate matches in the left and right images are evaluated by computing the correlation between a window of pixels centred on each edge [97]. The matching can also be based on stochastic modelling, which can take under consideration the spatial intra and intercorrelation of the stereo images [72]. The re-projection transform maps the matched points onto the road coordinate system. For this purpose it is necessary to know the exact relationship among the camera, vehicle and road coordinate systems. Under the assumption of a flat road, this reprojection process is quite straightforward (triangulation transform). In the case of general road conditions, however, the road geometry has to be estimated first in order to derive the re-projection transform from the camera to road coordinate systems. This estimation requires the exact knowledge of the state of the vehicle (yaw rate, vehicle speed, steering angle, etc.), which can be provided by appropriate sensors of the vehicle. Using this information, the road geometry can be estimated from visual data [65] [21].

2.4 Object Detection

2.4.11 Inverse perspective mapping

A promising approach in real-time object detection from video images is to remove the inherent perspective effect from acquired single or stereo images. The perspective effect relates differently 3D points on the road (world) coordinate system with 2D pixels on the image plane, depending on their distance from the camera. This effect associates different information content to different image pixels. Thus, road markings or objects of the same size appear smaller in the image as they move away from the camera coordinate system. The inverse perspective mapping aims at inverting the perspective effect, forcing homogeneous distribution of information within the image plane.

In order to be able to remove the perspective effect it is essential to know the image acquisition structure with respect to the road coordinates (camera position, orientation, etc.) and the road geometry (the flat-road assumption highly simplifies the problem). The inverse perspective mapping can be applied to stereovision [3], by re-mapping both right and left images into a common (road) domain. Using this approach, the localization of the lane and the detection of generic obstacles on the road can be performed without any 3Dworld reconstruction. The difference of the re-mapped views transforms relatively square obstacles into two neighbouring triangles corresponding to the vertical boundaries of the object, which can be easily detected on a polar histogram of the difference image.

2.4.12 3D modelling and forward mapping

The previous approaches reflect attempts to invert the 3D projection for a sequence of images and reconstruct the actual (world) spatial arrangement and motion of objects. The class of model-based techniques takes a different approach. It tries to solve the analysis task by carrying out an iterative synthesis with prediction error feedback using spatial-temporal world models. Model based approaches employ a parameterized 3D vehicle model for both its structural (shape) characteristics and its motion [17] [34]. Considering first a stationery camera, two major problems must be solved, namely the model matching and the motion estimation. The model matching process aims at finding the best match between the observed image and the 3D model projected onto the camera plane. This step is essentially a pose identification process, which derives the 3D position of the vehicle relative to the camera coordinates, based on 2D projections. The vehicle model often assumes straight line segments represented by their length and mid point location [60]. The line segments extracted from the image are matched to the model segments projected on the 2D camera plane. The matching can be based on the optimization of distance measures between the observation and the model; the Mahalanobis distance is used in [60]. The motion estimation process is based on models that describe the vehicle motion. The motion parameters of this model are estimated using a time recursive estimation process. For instance, the maximum a posteriori (MAP) estimator is employed in [60], whereas the extended Kalman filter is used in [90]. The estimation of motion and shape parameters can be combined in a more general (overall) state estimation process [90].

In the case of a moving camera, the changing views of objects during self or ego-motion reveal different aspects of the 3D geometry of objects and their surrounding environment.

Chapter 2

It becomes obvious that knowledge about the structure of the environment and the dynamics of motion are relevant components in real-time vision. In a computerized system, generic models of objects from the real world can be stored as three-dimensional structures carrying visible features at different spatial positions relative to their center of gravity. From the ego-motion dynamics, the relative position of the moving vehicle and its camera can be inferred. From this knowledge and applying the laws of forward projection (which is done much more easily than the inverse), the position and orientation of visual features in the image can be matched to those of the projected model [22] [23] [85]. In a different form, [22] models the remaining difference image from two consecutive frames after ego-motion compensation as a Markov random field (MRF) that incorporates the stochastic model of the hypothesis that a pixel is either static (background) or mobile (vehicle). The MRF also induces spatial and temporal smoothness constraints. The optimization of the energy function of the resulting Gibbs posterior distribution provides the motion-detection map at every pixel [85].

The dynamic consideration of a world model allows not only the computation of present vehicle positions, but also the computation of the effects of each component of the relative state vector on the vehicle position. This information can be maintained and used for estimating future vehicle positions. The partial derivatives for the parameters of each object at its current spatial position are collected in the Jacobian matrix as detailed information for interpreting the observed image. The ego-motion dynamics can be computed from the actuators of the moving vehicle. The dynamics of other moving obstacles can be modeled by stochastic disturbance variables. For simplicity, the motion of obstacles can be decomposed into translation and rotation over their center of gravity. Having this information, we can proceed with a prediction of the vehicle and obstacles states for the next time instant, when new measurements are taken.

If the cycle time of the measurement and control process is small and the state of the object is well known, the discrepancy between prediction and measurement should be small. Therefore, a linear approximation to the non-linear equations of the model should be sufficient for capturing the essential inter-relationships of the estimation process [22].

Moreover, for linear models the recursive state estimation is efficiently performed through least-square processes. Thus, the spatial state estimation through vision can be performed through recursive least squares estimation and Kalman filtering schemes, where the Jacobian matrix reflects the observed image variation. By applying this scheme to each object in the environment in parallel, an internal representation of the actual environment can be maintained in the interpretation process, by prediction error feedback [22]. A Kalman filter can be used to predict the vector of the state estimates based on the vectors of measurements and control variables. The measurement equation has to be computed only in the forward direction, from state variables (3D world) to measurement space (image plane). This approach avoids the ill-posed approximation of the non-unique inverse projection transform, through the fusion of dynamic models (that describe spatial motion) with 3D shape models (that describe spatial distribution of visual features). The forward projection mapping is easily evaluated under the flat-road model [22].

Other road models, including the Hill-and-Dale, Zero-Bank and Modified Zero-Bank models have been considered along with the inverse and/or forward mapping [76] [23] [104].

2.5 Color Vision - Short Overview

The study of the perception of color is historically intertwined with the study of the physical nature of light. The early discoveries in optics were made on the basis of direct observation, sometimes confounding the effects of perception with the physical nature of light.

The very pioneers in this research area [8] were Newton with his color wheel (which resembles a section through the HSI cone), Young with "On the theory of light and colors" [116], Brewster with the first theory stating that three properly chosen colors of light when mixed in careful proportions are all that is necessary to reproduce all color sensations (i.e. metameric substitution) [9], Helmholtz with "On the theory of compound colours" [107], Grassman who invented vector and tensor algebra demonstrating that for every spectral color there exists some other opponent color in the spectrum which when mixed with the first color in the correct proportions will produce white light [39] and finally Maxwell with "Experiments on colour, as perceived by the eye, with remarks on colour–blindness" [73].

First Maxwell defined the equations of light acting like a wave and then Einstein succeeded in showing that light also behaves as a particle, a photon. Each photon carries a particular packet, or quantum, of energy which is related to the wavelength of the light in Maxwell equation. These quanta of energy are often considered to be one dimensional numbers. In fact, it can be shown that a single photon cannot be represented as a one-dimensional number. The second dimension is commonly thought as a phase angle or as a polar orientation.

A light source will emit photons with various specific energy quanta depending on the potential energy changes in the electron configurations in the atomic structure of the light emitting substance. The resulting light spectrum is usually not uniform, since either the source or the transport medium usually favour parts of the spectrum while absorbing the others. The reflecting surface has its own absorption spectrum. Altogether they cause that the light reaching the eye from a certain surface is composed of a distribution of photons of various energy quantum values. This distribution is interpreted during the process of visual perception and it is assigned a single subjective value - a color. Colors do not exist independently, they a by-product of perception.

2.5.1 Mapping the Spectrum onto Perceptual Color Space

As Maxwell, Helmholz and many others have shown, a variety of spectral distributions of light can produce perceptions of color that are indistinguishable from one another. The visual perceptual system is thus mapping a high-dimensional input, the distribution of energy values of the photons arriving at each point of the retina, onto a low dimensional

Chapter 2

output where each point in the visual scene is assigned a single color. Obviously, information is being lost in the process, but it seems reasonable to consider that the visual system tries to preserve as much as possible from the useful information.

The characteristics of the spectrum of light have been closely and carefully studied. However, when it comes to perception of color and the representation of the color spaces there are still enough questions left without an answer [8]. Maybe the most important of them is how many dimensions should the color space have? Until the work of Neitz and colleagues (1990-1993), it was thought that the human retina has three types of cones. If the response function for each cone is linearized with respect to each other and the resultant color is a linear combination of cone outputs and no other information (like position of the cone) is used, than the resulting space has to have three dimensions. Recent research suggests that all prerequisites do not hold. The work of Vrhel, Gershon and Iwan (1994) suggest that at least four principal components are necessary to reduce and than reproduce complex spectral data from real world with reasonable accuracy. This result is an indication that the perceptual color space has at least 4 dimensions. In fact, Vrhel's analysis notes that substantial accuracy is once again gained when a fifth principal component is added as a basis vector for these reflectance spectra.

2.5.2 Color Spaces used in Computer Vision

Early color spaces had only two components. They largely ignored blue light because the added complexity of a 3-component process provided much less of a marginal increase in fidelity than the jump from monochrome to 2-component color. Some examples are RG for early Technicolor film and RGK for early color printing.

In computer vision, color spaces are mostly limited to 3 dimensions. Not only because of performance consideration, but also because of another practical reason. Currently the overwhelming majority of imaging devices are built around RGB sensors (either using Bayer patterns or optical 3 CDD systems). Therefore the source image is mostly represented in the 3 dimensional RGB color space for color acquisition systems. A lot of research has focused around RGB color space and derivates from it, like ratios between the three primary colors. Still the RGB space has one major disadvantage as it does not have a single axis to represent the color. When speaking of color in RGB, one has to take into account either all three components or some combination of them. This limitation is solved in other color spaces. One advantage of the RGB space is that since most source images are represented in it, no further conversion is necessary for the processing.

The CMYK (cyan, magenta, yellow and black) space uses subtractive color mixing as in the printing process, describing what kind of inks need to be applied so the light reflected from them produces a given color. It is from the research point of view just a complementary color space to RBG. All advantages and disadvantages of RGB space are encountered in the CMYK space as well.

YIQ is used in NTSC television broadcasts for historical reasons. YIQ stores a luminance value with two chrominance values, corresponding approximately to the amounts of blue and red in the color. It corresponds closely to the YUV scheme used in PAL

2.5 Color Vision - Short Overview

television except that the YIQ color space is rotated with 33 grades with respect to the YUV color space. The YDbDr scheme used by SECAM television is rotated differently. All of these three spaces are optimized for the way color is transmitted and displayed in television and are not largely used in computer vision in this form. However since they are efficient for the compression of signals, some of their derivatives are used in image compression algorithms. For example, YPbPr is a scaled version of YUV. It is most commonly seen in its digital form, YCbCr, used widely in video and image compression schemes such as MPEG and JPEG.

HSV is often used in publishing and new media by content creators because it is often more natural to think about a color in terms of hue and saturation than in terms of additive or subtractive color components. HSV stores a hue value, a saturation value and an intensity value. HLS is quite similar to HSV, with lightness replacing the intensity value. Both color spaces eliminate the major problem of RGB by representing the color on a single axis (Hue). They have their specific disadvantages that derive from the fact that no physical imaging device is supporting them. This leads to conversion formulas that have an impact on both the definition of space and the accuracy of values that can be derived from the source RGB image as shown in [40]. The HSV/HLS representations suffer from some problems, such as presence of unstable singularities and non-uniform distributions of their components, as described by [55]. Nevertheless, they can be more intuitive than the RGB representation, and could reveal image features which are not clearly visible in this representation. Therefore they have been widely adopted by the scientific community doing research on color computer vision.

The problems of all color spaces presented until now led to research in the direction of a color spaces more suitable for image processing [40]. Still their adoption is very limited and therefore will not be presented here.

2.5.3 Active Research in Color Vision for Active Driver Assistance Systems

The major research areas in which color vision proved its specific advantages in the automotive domain are (i) detecting and interpreting the specific color manmade structures present on the road (like yellow markings, road signs, etc.), (ii) shadow detection and removal, (iii) object detection and (iv) detection and removal of the surrounding background based on its color.

Detection and interpretation of the specific color manmade structures present on the road is a very large subject that includes at least traffic sign recognition, information-shield recognition, yellow marking recognition, controlled environment segmentation, etc. Mostly all of these methods used two steps: segmentation of the image in some color space (RGB, HSI and YUV are the most used) and consequently, recognition of the objects using form and color information. Color segmentation is treated below, along with the object detection. Since this thesis does not include any of these methods, except for the yellow lane recognition (and in this case there are very few available references), these methods will no be presented in detail.

Chapter 2

Shadow detection and removal remains a difficult task as long as the scene geometry, composition of the materials and the complete characterization of the flux of light through the scene are not known in detail. In the automotive environment all of these prerequisites are not met. Therefore distinguishing shadows from changes in material color or reflectance remains a very challenging task. The first solutions were based on simple thresholding of the intensity (or brightness) of the local image areas [78] [110]. Later, when color processing was available on a larger scale, it became obvious that the color information is a crucial key in the shadow recognition algorithms. One of the most extensive papers on this area is [35]. Both color information and geometry are analysed as input of the shadow recognition process. The color space used in [35] is the RGB space. Spectral responses are computed using ratios between R, G und B components. Another method of detecting shadows using color information, but this time in the HSI/V spaces is the one used in [94]. The property used, that shadows only modify the I component of the space, applies to chromatic surfaces, but does not always hold on concrete (generally speaking monochromatic) surfaces, where all three components of the space suffer significant modifications.

Object detection in automotive scenes using color is relative new. Segmenting images based on color information has been around since the first color images were acquired. Still, bringing a color segmentation algorithm to fulfil the real time requirements of the automotive industry was a difficult task. The first step in recognizing vehicles moving on the road surface is to segment the image - in other words to classify each pixel in an image into one of a discrete number of color classes. The leading approaches to accomplishing this task include linear color thresholding, nearest neighbour classification, color space thresholding and probabilistic methods. Linear color thresholding works by partitioning the color space with linear boundaries (e.g. planes in 3 dimensional spaces). A particular pixel is then classified according to which partition it lies in. This method is convenient for learning systems such as neural networks, or multivariate decision trees [10]. A second approach is to use nearest neighbour classification. Typically several hundred preclassified exemplars are employed, each having a unique location in the color space and an associated classification. To classify a new pixel, a list of the K nearest exemplars is found, then the pixel is classified according to the largest proportion of classifications of the neighbours [13]. Both linear thresholding and nearest neighbour classification provide good results in terms of classification accuracy, but do not provide realtime performance using "off the shelf" hardware. Another approach is to use a set of constant thresholds defining a color class as a rectangular block in the color space [50]. This approach performs well, but is unable to take advantage of potential dependencies between the color space dimensions. A derivative of the constant thresholding has been implemented in hardware by Newton Laboratories. Their product provides color tracking data at realtime rates, but is significantly more expensive than "pure software approaches" on general purpose hardware. A final related approach is to store a discretized version of the entire joint probability distribution [92]. So, for example, to check whether a particular pixel is a member of the color class, its individual color components are used as indices to a multidimensional array. When the location is looked up in the array the returned value

2.5 Color Vision - Short Overview

indicates probability of membership. This technique enables a modelling of arbitrary distribution volumes and membership can be checked with reasonable efficiency. The approach also enables the user to represent unusual membership volumes (e.g. cones or ellipsoids) and thus capture dependencies between the dimensions of the color space. The primary drawback to this approach is the high memory cost for speed the entire probability matrix must be present in RAM-. Once the color image is segmented, the obtained regions are identified as objects based on their form, position, motion or structure. The algorithms are similar to the greyscale algorithms that were detailed in 2.4.

Background detection and substraction is used in many driver assistance approaches mostly under two different forms. The first is to "black-out" the detected background (render it insignificant by setting the pixels to a neutral value; black or white for example are commonly used). Consequently, the algorithms process the image normally. The latter is to used regions of interest in the algorithm definition so that the algorithm does not process the detected background. Background detection relies normally on multiple clues like texture, color, position in the image, etc. Since the background detection is not treated in this work, the existing state of the art methods will not be presented in detail.

Chapter 2

3 Image Segmentation in HSI, Lane and Object Recognition

3.1 Generics

3.1.1 Motivation

Color vision was around for more than a few decades. Mostly due to hardware limitations and sensor costs the applications in the automotive domain remained very limited.

Nowadays both limitations are almost overcome by the development of hardware. The mobile phone market is driving down the costs for color imaging sensors and optical devices (most cameras for such mobile device are supporting the VGA standard and a limited zoom factor) while current embedded systems reached computing powers that were until shortly hard to imagine except for personal computers (current low-power MIPS based processors running at 300 MHz - 1Ghz use 0.5 - 3 Watts, e.g. AMD Alchemy/Geode, Intel XScale or Motorola PowerPC solutions).

In the near future, both hardware and sensor costs limitations will be made redundant and the color vision sensors together with the processing hardware will be largely available. This will make them a common choice for comfort oriented driver assistance applications. Even more, the automotive industry in Europe is increasingly faced with safety regulations. In order to comply with them, the OEMs will need to integrate sensors able to perform classification of objects and to use multisensorial based approaches. In both these scenarios the color camera will be a better choice than a greyscale one, provided that the research and development of the processing algorithms will be able to keep the pace with the market developments.

The current research on color vision for the automotive industry is limited as it can be seen from the number of papers presented at the major conferences in the last years. This work tries to fill in the gap by developing a complete, stand alone vision system targeting automotive applications. Its primary focus is the development of novel methods for traffic lane detection and object detection (cars, trucks) based on the color information. Due to the multitude of existing solutions based on greyscale vision, a second focus is the study of the improvements for already existing methods using the additional information provided by the saturation and hue components. Besides color vision, another focus for this work is the cognitive approach taken, instead of the typical mathematical models. The scene is first interpreted based on existing knowledge about the environment and only at the very end is the 3D conversion performed. This allows for more flexible and less demanding requirements regarding the camera calibration and for an easier future

Chapter 3

development of the system.

3.2 Image Segmentation Based on SI Metrics

3.2.1 HSI Space Characteristics

The color space chosen is the (H)ue (S)aturation (I)ntensity. The Hue Saturation Value space is very similar and can be substituted to the HSI without changes in the described algorithms. The minimal gain due to the improved contrast in the value component is not noticeable. The computation of the intensity has the advantage of mediating the noises present in a singular axis in the original RGB space (particularly noticeable in case of 3CCD systems). The transformation from the source RGB space to the HSI space is performed with the well known formulas [69]:

$$I = \frac{R+G+B}{3} \tag{3.1}$$

$$S = 1 - \frac{3}{R+G+B} * min(R,G,B) \tag{3.2}$$

$$H = \arccos\left(\frac{\frac{1}{2}*[(R-G)+(R-B)]}{\sqrt{(R-G)^2+(R-B)(G-B)}}\right) \tag{3.3}$$

if $B > G$, then $H = 2*\pi - H$.

The conversion process from RGB to HSI is similar to a transformation from rectangular to polar coordinates. One first places a new axis in the RGB space between $(0,0,0)$ and $(1,1,1)$. This axis passes through all the achromatic points (i.e. those with $R = G = B$), and is therefore called the achromatic axis. One then chooses a function I(R, G, B) which calculates the brightness, luminance or lightness of color. The form chosen for I defines the shape of the iso-brightness surfaces. The iso-brightness surface K contains all the points with a brightness of I_k, i.e. all the points satisfying the relation $I(R,B,G) = I_k$. These iso-brightness surfaces are then projected onto a plane perpendicular to the achromatic axis and intersecting it at the origin, called the chromatic plane as it contains all the color information. The hue and saturation or chroma coordinates of each point are then determined within the plane, where the hue corresponds to the angular coordinate around the achromatic axis, and the saturation or chroma corresponds to a distance from the achromatic axis.

To visualise the shape of the resulting space, the points of each iso-brightness surface K are projected onto a chromatic plane intersecting the achromatic axis at K. The solid corresponding to a color space is constructed out of the sub-regions of each chromatic plane containing projected points. The form of this solid depends on the brightness function [40].

The common representation of the HSI space found in literature is the double cone representation. Due to the fact that this representation does not cover the complete

3.2 Image Segmentation Based on SI Metrics

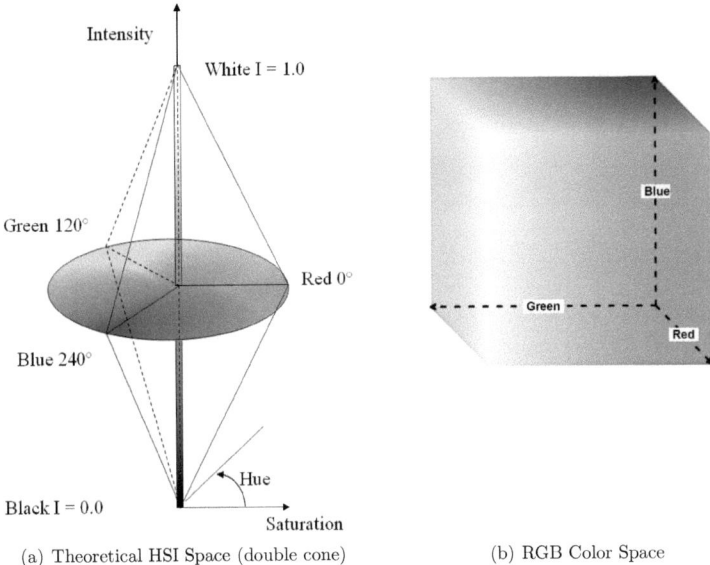

(a) Theoretical HSI Space (double cone)   (b) RGB Color Space

Figure 3.1: Theoretical HSI Space and RGB Spaces

HSI space as obtained from the conversion formulas, it is often extended to a cylindrical representation.

The sensor of choice in typical automotive applications is an RGB sensor (CCD or CMOS) with an 8 bit signal for each channel, i.e. the RGB 24 bit format. The HSI image has to be obtained from the RGB one by applying the conversion formulas. Since the R, G, B elements are represented on 8 bit, they can take integer values in the range 0 to 255. Therefore the transformation to HSI coordinates will lead to a subset of the theoretical HSI color space. The form of this subset of the HSI space is relevant in order to understand its properties.

To plot the form of the HSI space, all 256^3 possible (R, G, B) input triplets were generated and then transformed to HSI using the formulas in (3.1) - (3.3). The three axes of the space are $X = S * cos(H)$, $Y = S * sin(H)$, $Z = I$.

In fig. 3.2 is presented the form of the HSI Space projected on the ZY plane (Z axis is Intensity, Y axis is Saturation * sin(Hue)). As it can be seen, if in the upper part of the figure the values converge to the I = 255, S = 0 point. In the lower part the values are not converging to a defined point, but are spread in the theoretical cylindrical space. This

41

Chapter 3

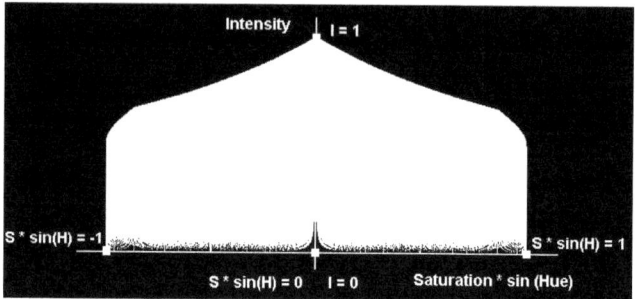

Figure 3.2: HSI Space Obtained from 24 Bit RGB

particularity of the HSI Space could be also formulated "for the lower intensity region, the saturation values do not converge to 0, but are exhibiting high values".

As seen from fig. 3.2, one particularity is that for the upper half of the space (intensity values higher that 0.5) the saturation will converge respecting the known conical representation. For the lower half of the space (intensity values lower than 0.5) this property does not hold anymore and the saturation takes large values.

Due to the integer input values, the obtained HSI points are sparse for the low intensity region (as it can be also seen from the lower part of the fig. 3.2). For example the RGB triplet (0, 1, 1) gives $S = 1$ (maximum possible value) while the triplet (1, 1, 1) gives 0 (minimum possible value). Both triplets represent very dark (almost black) image elements that are practically indistinguishable for the human eye. These extreme changes in the saturation element are affecting only dark image areas. This is another important particularity of the HSI values generated from digital RGB images.

There are multiple ways to deal with these issues. One is to accept as default in the algorithms that if I is below a certain threshold, than the S component is either invalid or has higher values than expected. This leads to somehow more complicated algorithms, but their complexity remains manageable. Another solution is to replace the formulas in the low-intensity cases with predefined values for the saturation. This will not require any special handling in the algorithms, but the used space even if related to HSI, will not be identical anymore, therefore the solution cannot be compared to the ones based on the HSI/HSV representations.

3.2.2 Projection of Road Scenes in HSI Space

In order to be able to perform a segmentation in the HSI space, at least the following questions must be answered:

(i) Where are located the features to extract in the HSI space?

(ii) Which of the 3 dimensions of the space are most relevant to the segmentation process?

3.2 Image Segmentation Based on SI Metrics

Figure 3.3: Sample Image and its H, S, I components

(iii) What is the function that can be used as weighting function for the image points?
(iv) What is(are) the value(s) of thresholds in the segmentation process?

In order to answer these four questions some characteristics of the typical road scenes in the HSI space are analyzed. Most of the analysed scenes are highway traffic scenarios. The reason is that the system was designed for a first application as a sensor in a highway assistant based on a multi-sensor fusion approach. The analysis is performed on a typical scene. It is done gradually starting with the intensity information, then saturation, their combination and finally extended to the whole HSI space. The results are then generalized and applied to different illumination conditions and different traffic scenes.

The data from fig. 3.3 is analyzed in the next sections. A low contrast image, with respect to color information, was chosen on purpose to show the robustness of the methods. The saturation values had to be multiplied by 4 (saturated to 255 in case of overflow) for the sake of readability on printed material.

Chapter 3

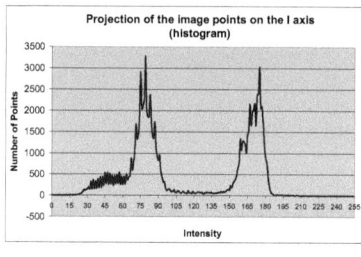
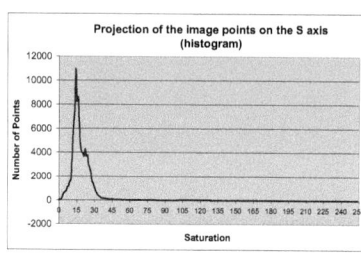

(a) Intensity (b) Saturation

Figure 3.4: Histograms of the I, S Values of Image Points

Looking at the three components of the color image in fig. 3.3, the following conclusions can be drawn:

- intensity carries the most information (this comes to no surprise since most of the infrastructure is monochromatic and the human eye uses form and position besides color to identify and track objects in its field of view)

- saturation when well defined has small values (the remarks about the artificially saturated dark pixels from the previous section are confirmed on the saturation image)

- hue data alone is extremely hard to interpret even for a person who has already seen the original picture (hue alone does not carry enough information, if combined with the saturation the image would have been recognizable).

Unfortunately this situation is commonly encountered in automotive scenes. This is also one of the main reasons that make color processing seem not to give any advantage over the more common encountered greyscale approaches. In the next paragraphs I and S are analyzed separately and then together to find out how they can be combined to deliver better information than the intensity alone.

Projecting the Points on the I Axis

One observation has to be made before starting the analysis. The simple arithmetic mean used to compute I from the original R,G,B values has the tendency to decrease the contrast of the obtained greyscale figure. This effect is normally noticed as a more compact histogram. Other algorithms (namely luminance, brightness and value) have been tried in order to avoid reaching false conclusions. Still, the conclusions remained the same in all cases. Therefore, the arithmetic mean is used for I in this work.

It can be observed from fig. 3.4(a) that the task of a greyscale algorithm is far from being an easy one. The regions representing the vehicles in the scene are overlapping

3.2 Image Segmentation Based on SI Metrics

with the ones carrying the lane marking information and with those that are belonging to the road information. There is only one region on the histogram that has a relatively clear correspondence in the picture. It is situated at the right of the histogram around the values of 180. It corresponds to the lane markings. Still, the two vehicles having reflex-silver metallic color (the near Golf 4 and the far VW Transporter Van) have their interference materialized in the two secondary spikes with intensity values around 160, respectively 170-175. If a white car was present in the proximity of the camera this property would loose its validity. This makes it necessary to take into account other information as well (like picture position of the points) in order to be able to extract some useful data. If the illumination conditions change –in our case scene illumination even if reduced it is still diffuse, i.e. almost optimal– or a variation in the camera gain/exposure is applied the values will change significantly and sometimes even the general form of the histogram is affected.

Intensity values alone cannot be generally used to make a segmentation of the image that is able to separate the objects from the road and lane markings even if some information is already present. In few particular cases when all objects are significantly brighter than the road and darker than the markings, the segmentation may give some results, but generally the bright colored cars will mix with the lane markings while the dark ones will mix with the road. These cases can be solved using the position in the picture or some models for the environment, but this is already too complex for the intended low level segmentation methods.

Projecting the points on the S Axis

The same problems arise with the projection on the S axis as can be seen in fig. 3.4(b). Moreover, the values of the saturation are all relatively low, so that observations like the secondary peaks make no sense. One can certainly say that saturation values alone are so noisy and low that they are almost unusable. Under better lightning conditions they become much better, still their meaning is harder to interpret than in the case of intensity values.

Few observations can be made. Since the saturation of any gray-like color is very low, its hue information is not only useless but also misleading. This can be clearly seen for the road information that has no well defined hue values, but mainly acquisition noise, ranging from green to blue. It is interesting to note that for bright regions the saturation values are not noisy, as it can be seen in fig. 3.2. This is in agreement with the double cone representation of the HSI space (see [87]).

Before moving to the analysis of the SI plane, the projections of the points on other lines in the SI plane were investigated. The situation is similar to the S and I axis. Moreover since they do not have a meaningful geometric interpretation in most cases it is more difficult to explain the results.

Chapter 3

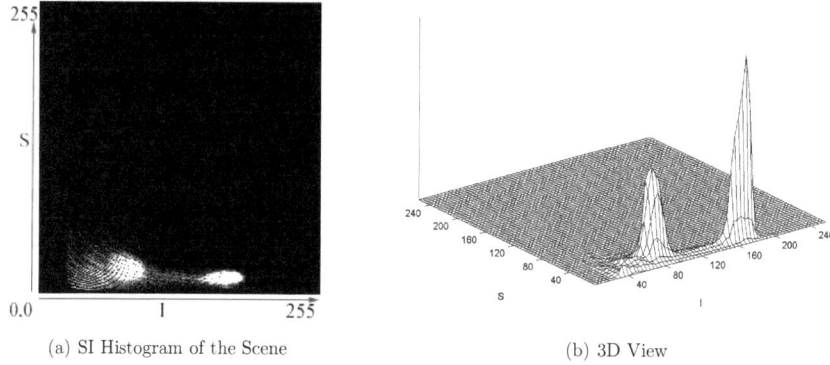

(a) SI Histogram of the Scene (b) 3D View

Figure 3.5: Saturation-Intensity Histogram of the Scene

Figure 3.6: Correspondence between the SI histogram and the original image

Using the SI Plane

Since S and I axis or other lines in the SI plane are not useful to segment the image in the intended way, the SI plane was being investigated. Fig. 3.5(a) presents the histogram in the SI plane. The chosen representation maps the brightest color to the highest peak into the histogram. This is sometimes easier to interpret than viewing the 3D plot from various angles (e.g. 3.5(b)). The first question was whether it would be possible to correlate the peaks from the SI histogram with the image objects. Fig. 3.6 shows the correspondence.

3.2 Image Segmentation Based on SI Metrics

The sky and the road generate the two major peaks labelled 2 and 4. The lane markings are situated in the same position as the sky peak, mostly in the lower region. The vehicles, road signs, road delimiters and the vegetation generate the rest of the secondary peaks that can be seen on the histogram (see fig. 3.2.2). This situation is common in all traffic scenes, due to the fact that the automotive infrastructure (in this case road and lane markings) is invariant.

Figure 3.7: Example of SI footprint of small chromatic objects

The scene in fig. 3.7 is an example of how a chromatic object generates a distinct peak in the SI plane. As opposed to fig. 3.6, where the contrast was low and the objects had very dark surfaces, the truck on the right lane has a relatively large red surface and a clear contrast. Correspondingly, it generates a distinct peak that can be seen above the projection of the rest of the figure. Another relevant aspect is that the green vegetation present on both sides of the highway generates a large footprint in the SI plane, overlapped with the one of the road.

Figure 3.8: Example of SI footprint of large chromatic objects

In fig. 3.8 the ego vehicle closes on the truck and the footprint of the truck shows up as a large, distinct peak in the SI plane. Since the truck surface covers the trees on the

Chapter 3

right side, the footprint of the vegetation in the SI plane is reduced as compared to fig. 3.7. In 3.2.5 there are more traffic scene analyzed. They have different illuminations, road surfaces and scene compositions. Still, the basic elements of the SI histogram are presented, showing that there is possible to segment these images using the SI plane for the segmentation process.

One may note that the regions on the SI histogram do overlap partially. It is not possible to always have a distinct SI histogram that can offer a good image segmentation using no additional information. In controlled environments it may be possible, but the real world applications may need to use more than a basic image segmentation to obtain the objects in the image.

3.2.3 SI Metrics

As seen from 3.2.1 the cars, lane markings, road and sky cluster in the SI plane. This makes it possible to classify the image points, based on their distances in the SI plane to the class average, into the classes. A function is used to weight the image points and afterwards using one or more thresholds they can be assigned to some classes like markings, road and so on.

This subsection presents several weighting functions [1] based on their suitability for the segmentation of image points. Besides its accurate segmentation the ideal weighting function should be simple enough to allow a fast computation. This means that, in the optimal case, only integer arithmetic is used in the computation.

It comes as no surprise that the well-known Euclidian metric can be used in most of the cases. One point is chosen and the distances for others points are computed with respect to its SI values (S_p, I_p) using the well-known formula (3.4). Choosing the reference point is one of the key aspects of the metric. In our case the point can belong neither to the road (S_r, I_r) nor to the markings (S_m, I_m) since they are pretty different from average SI values. One solution would be to use a combination of them as in (3.5) or to choose a point that normally belongs to cars (for example the high saturation, average intensity point that has S = 255, I = 128).

$$F_1 = \sqrt{(S - S_p)^2 + (I - I_p)^2} \qquad (3.4)$$
$$F_2 = \min(F_1(S_r, I_r), F_1(S_m, I_m)) \qquad (3.5)$$

The metric in (3.6) is just a fast variant of the Euclidian metric. Since the values for S and I range between 0 and 255 the square root can be replaced (the accuracy decreases) by division with an integer. The value that brings all the possible output in the [0..255] interval is $255^2 * 2/255 = 510$. In order to be able to obtain an acceptable resolution of the metric output, the divider has to be computed dynamically as detailed in section 3.2.6.

---

[1] The "metric" term is used here in a relaxed notation, without giving both points as function parameters. If the weighting function has the mathematical properties of a metric, then it is called so. If not, then it will be simply called "weighting function".

3.2 Image Segmentation Based on SI Metrics

F_3 was used in this work since all its operations can be executed in integer arithmetic. The metric works well in those areas that differ from the road or lane markings. Due to shadows present under the car, the metric usually succeeds in extracting an almost horizontal area at the bottom of the cars. The body of the car is not always extracted due to the way the reference point was chosen and its distant SI values from the tyres.

$$F_3 = \frac{(S - S_p)^2 + (I - I_p)^2}{Divider} \quad (3.6)$$

One weighting function that is particularly efficient for the extraction of lane markings is (3.7). It performs well when S has very low and I relatively high values; white lane markings are the image elements that own this property. For the extraction of yellow lane markings the function can be changed to (3.8) where S_y is the typical saturation for the yellow markings. It depends on how strong the yellow footprint is in the image (related to the reflectiveness of the marking), one the direction of the light, on day/night condition and so on. A few lane marking points were chosen for each frame and their averaged S,I values were used to test the results of applying the weighting function.

$$F_4 = \frac{(255 - I) * S}{256} \quad (3.7)$$

$$F_5 = \frac{abs(S_y - S) * (255 - I)}{256} \quad (3.8)$$

Shadows pose relatively small problems unless combined with direct illumination (sunrise/sunset in front of the camera). In this case the contrast of the scene decreases significantly and the color information is hardly usable. All scene pixels tend to have extremely small S values. Applying a metric that equally weights the S and I components makes the elimination of shadows only by a simple thresholding impossible. A solution was found by using a metric that weights S and I differently like in (3.9).

$$F_6 = \frac{W_1 * (S - S_p)^2 + W_2 * (I - I_p)^2}{Divider * (W_1 + W_2)}, W1 > W2 \quad (3.9)$$

The metric F_6 (3.9) performs much better for the extraction of road/lane marking information than any of the presented metrics for the case of strong shadows. Still the problem remains not completely solved. The problem of shadows can be only solved by using a higher representation of the environment.

3.2.4 Effects of HSI Space Irregularities

Once the weighting functions are defined, it is important to see how they are performing in case of lower intensity values (both HSI Space particularities presented in 3.2.1 are related to lower intensity values). The metric F_3 is analyzed here, since it was the one most used in this work. In order to be able to identify the pixels, in F_3 one has to choose

Chapter 3

(a) Scene 1   (b) Scene 2

Figure 3.9: Overimposed Results using the Weighting Function F_3

the reference values for S_p and I_p in such a way that the distance of the processed pixel to the reference point will be minimal.

In the case of chromatic elements the $(S - S_p)^2$ member in F_3 dictates a big value for S_p.

In the case of very dark elements the saturation values are usually high. In this case the $(S - S_p)^2$ member in F_3 also dictates a big values for S_p. In practice, there are very few pixels in which the three RGB components are having the same values and therefore the saturation will be 0.

This is a very important result, because it shows that the classification of both relevant image features can be done with a single weighting function that looks for high saturation values and low intensity values in the HSI space.

The metric F_3 from (3.6) was used extensively in this work. It is very fast, if properly implemented its computation takes about the same time as a standard traversal of the image using two standard for loops. An example of applying this metric relative to the point having S = 255, I = 128 and after plotting all values that are lower than 170 is shown in fig. 3.9(b). The chosen point bears on purpose no relation to the actual SI values in the picture and the chosen metric is the fastest one (not the most accurate one). This proves the robustness of the method. The metric correctly extracts a significant number of points from all objects and close landscape and extracts practically only isolated points from the road or lane markings. This behaviour was encountered in the overwhelming majority of the conducted tests. The real difficulty here is to choose the proper threshold before making the segmentation. One option is to use the threshold that eliminates both road and lane markings, i.e. to compute the threshold from the average SI values of the road. Another possibility is to use the reference point on an already detected tyre; this will decrease the number of points that belong to the outer environment, but will increase the number of points that are detected in the lower part of the vehicle. This is

3.2 Image Segmentation Based on SI Metrics

the way the metric was applied in object detection algorithms. Composed metrics (best result of more metrics) even if very promising from a researcher's point of view, are less practicable due to their high computation costs. To illustrate this point, the example of extracting all lane markings (white and yellow) before a classification takes place based on their hue values is offered.

In this work the metrics F_3 and F_4 are used. They were chosen due to their simplicity. The possible parameters of two formulas are (i) one reference point and (ii) one divider. In order to improve their sensitivity those two parameters can be dynamically computed for every frame. The threshold can also be adjusted dynamically to counteract the frequent changes in the illumination that are typical for automotive scenes.

3.2.5 Projections of Typical Traffic Scenes on the SI Plane

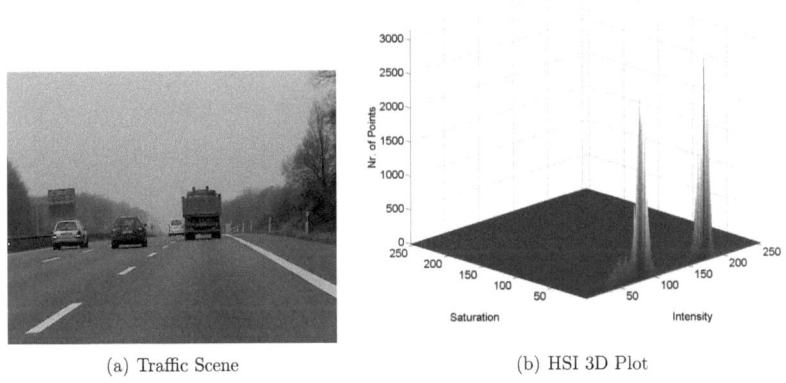

(a) Traffic Scene   (b) HSI 3D Plot

Figure 3.10: Normal 3 lane highway scene

In what follows the conclusions from the previous subsections will be extended to cover the typical road scenes in various illumination conditions. The conclusions will lead later to the selection of the SI metric and will also show the need for the automatic adaptation of thresholds. Different weather conditions were not extensively presented here since they mostly affect the contrast of the image and not the image contents itself. Besides, presenting the whole spectrum of possible illumination and weather conditions exceeds the editorial space of this work.

The 3D histograms on the right side of the following figures are drawn as 3D heat like plots where the highest point values on the Z axis are mapped to bright red colors (warm) and the 0 values are mapped to blue colors (cold). In the saturated images (where the peak for I = 255 is singular), the histogram is not continuous around the highest peak.

51

Chapter 3

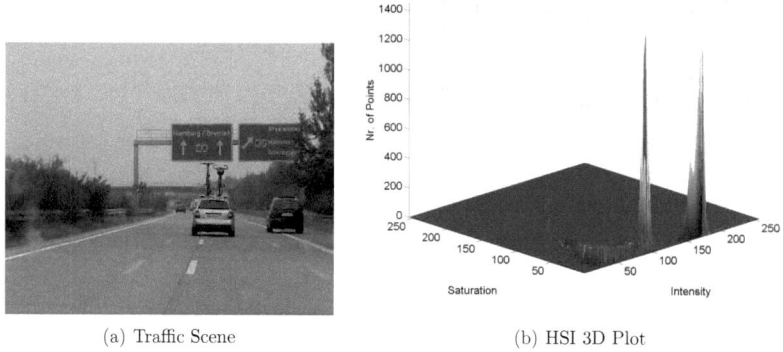

(a) Traffic Scene   (b) HSI 3D Plot

Figure 3.11: Low contrast, concrete surface

This results in a harder to see peak (due mostly to the imperfections in the plotting software), materialized on the histogram as a single vertical line, in most of the cases not continuous (plotting the line in 3D results in rounding errors that make some of the parts "invisible" for that particular viewing angle).

The already discussed scene in fig. 3.3 is the first presented. It is the reference to which the changes in other histograms are compared. The corresponding histogram in fig. 3.10(b) has as characteristic the very distinct peaks for sky and road and some lower intensity peaks for the vegetation and the vehicles present on the road. This gives already a first indication about the limits of the segmentation in SI coordinates: it may be very hard to distinguish the vehicles from the vegetation.

In the particular case of roads made out of concrete as exemplified in fig. 3.11(b), the contrast between the road and the sky is low. Due to the brighter concrete surface, in lower illumination conditions (diffuse illumination) the two peaks for road and sky are closer on the histogram, but still their position and the general form of the histogram remains the same. The traffic shield is individualized in the higher saturation peaks, while the A4 vehicle carrying the two bicycles generates a second peak (having greater saturation) above the sky peak.

If until now the analysed scenes had an average-to-low contrast, the scene in fig. 3.12(b) is "crystal clear". The result is visible also in the 3D histogram. The two main peaks are containing less than 800 points each (about 2-3 times less than for fig. 3.11(b)). The difference is noticeable in the extent of the two peaks, they extend more in the saturation. Another new element is given by the already noticeable peaks in the region with high saturation and low intensity. These are due to the large, dark car in the image. Especially the lower part of the car is generating a lot of artificially high saturated pixels, confirming

3.2 Image Segmentation Based on SI Metrics

the theoretical results in fig. 3.2.

The difference between fig. 3.12(b) and fig. 3.12(b) illustrates the need for a dynamic adaptation of the metric thresholds to the current image quality. Having static thresholds means that the area around the reference point of the metric containing the relevant points is static, or, as in this particular case the area of the base of the peak is almost 3 times bigger.

The scene in fig. 3.13(b) illustrates the opposite situation. The high and direct illumination is forcing the camera to reduce its contrast. The pixels of the sky cluster almost exclusively to the highest intensity position, which accounts for more than 5000 pixels in the image. In comparison, the other peaks seem small, but are still having the already known distribution with the road pixels clustering around $I = 100$, the dark vegetation accounting for the lower intensity elements and the two white cars and lane markings accounting for the rest of the peaks disposed between $I = 100$ and $I = 240$.

This histogram shows the need for a modality to compute the reference points for the metric dynamically. The road peak remained at about $I = 100$, but the sky shifted with more than 100 points to the upper-most intensity position. A reference point for the sky has to adapt itself to the new conditions in order to compensate the shift with more than 1/3 of the intensity range.

A similar situation occurs in the case when fog is obscuring the details as in fig. 3.14(a). This case shows how all image pixels covered by the fog tend to cluster in the higher intensity regions as seen in fig. 3.14(b). The form of the plot remains similar, with a second peak for the road pixels.

A very clear illustration of the possibility of using color in identifying the pixels that belong to some homogenously colored objects can be seen in fig. 3.15(b). The traffic

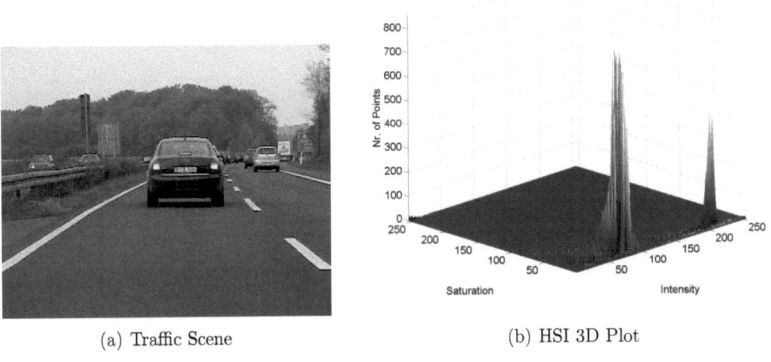

(a) Traffic Scene   (b) HSI 3D Plot

Figure 3.12: High contrast scene, close car

Chapter 3

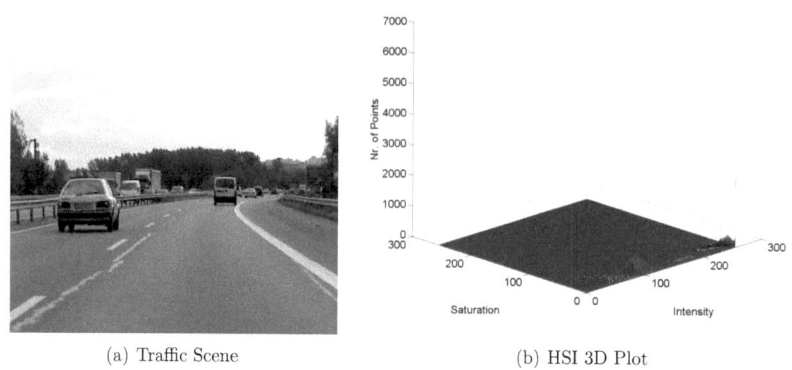

(a) Traffic Scene (b) HSI 3D Plot

Figure 3.13: Saturated image

shield generates a clearly distinct peak centred about I = 80, S = 100. The scene in fig. 3.15(b) shows also how the lane marking points group clearly from the sky points (the two peaks in the higher intensity region).

Summing up, the few examples led to the following conclusions:

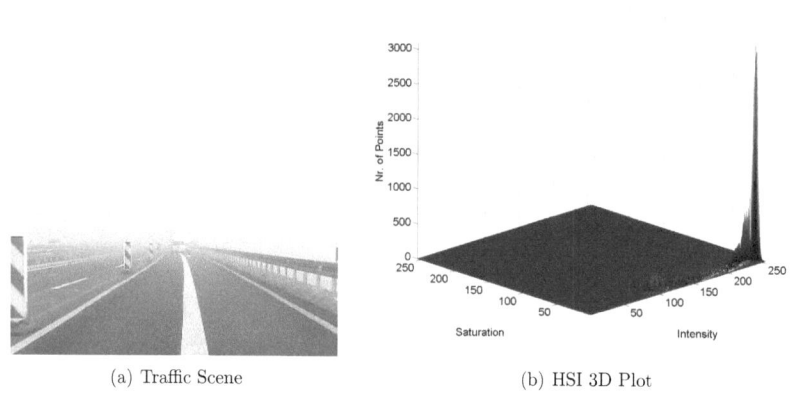

(a) Traffic Scene (b) HSI 3D Plot

Figure 3.14: Fog scene

3.2 Image Segmentation Based on SI Metrics

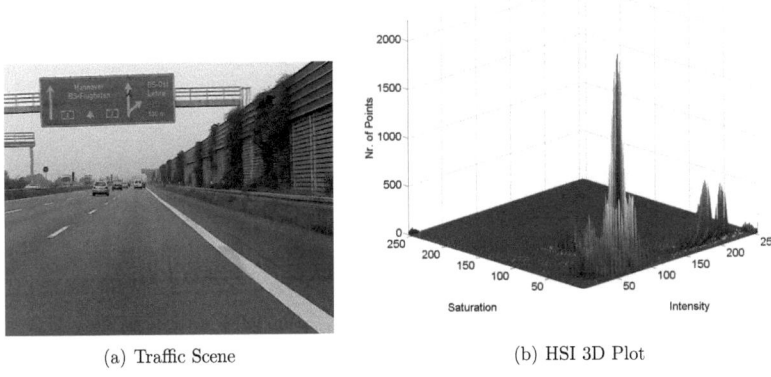

(a) Traffic Scene (b) HSI 3D Plot

Figure 3.15: Free highway, with traffic shield

- the pixels cluster in the SI plane in such a way that their classification in road/non-road classes becomes possible
- the objects that have a homogenous color will generate well individualized peaks on the SI histogram
- the peaks may be very compact or sparse depending on the illumination conditions (or the settings of the camera). Therefore using fixed thresholds to separate the SI plane will probably be of little use in real applications.
- it should be possible to use metrics similar to the Euclidian metric, since the SI space is a Euclidian one
- in a complete object-identification process, the position of the pixels in the picture as well as their specific form or properties (symmetry) are to be used in addition to the SI segmentation and clustering

3.2.6 Adaptive SI Metric Coefficients

The parametrizable elements for the function F_3 are:
- the interest point (center of measurement)
- the divider (e.g. for F_3 510 brings all output values within the range 0 .. 255 but also compresses the areas of interest within this range too much)
- the threshold which has to be used to decide if a point belongs to a class or not

The new form of the metric F_3 from (3.6) is show in (3.10). The main differences to (3.6) are:
- the addition of the reference point for the class to the function definition (in order to obtain consistent results, the reference point was computed once per frame and remained

Chapter 3

the same for all pixels of the frame)
 - the presence of the divider as a variable quantity (to ensure reproducible results it will be computed once for each frame).

$$F_3(S, I, S_p, I_p) = \frac{(S - S_p)^2 + (I - I_p)^2}{DynamicDivider}. \qquad (3.10)$$

Besides computing the divider dynamically, the threshold can also be determined dynamically. The algorithm requires two points (in SI plane). The first point should be chosen in such a way that it becomes a positive match from the metric (an "insider"), while the second should be chosen outside the relevant area in the SI plane (an "outsider").

Defining the "insider" and "outsider" points should pose no problem since driver assistance systems based on video identify the road and the lane markings. Therefore the road detection algorithm delivers a road region that can be used to allow for a selection of average road S,I values. Selecting an "outsider" would then be the same as specifying the average road values. Specifying an "insider" has to do with the scope of the detection algorithm which uses the metric. If a reference point for a lane marking is needed, then the point should be chosen to belong to a lane marking. The object detection algorithms will typically specify the point on the tyre of the car (a common image characteristic of all vehicles).

Having obtained both reference points, the metric is computed in such a way that the distance between the "insider" and "outsider" values is maximal (255). This is the same as saying that $F_3(S_o, I_o, S_i, I_i) = 255$. Factoring out the divider and replacing the metric value with 255 in 3.10, it yields the computation formula for the divider (3.11).

$$Divider(S_o, I_o, S_i, I_i) = \frac{(S_i - S_o)^2 + (I_i - I_o)^2}{255} \qquad (3.11)$$

In (3.11) the symbols mean: S_i, I_i saturation and intensity of the "insider" point. S_o, I_o for the pixel corresponding to the "outsider" (typically average values of the detected road surface).

The threshold defines the outer boundary of the positive matches. For each point that is evaluated the result obtained by apply the formula 3.10 to its S, I values is compared with the threshold. If it is smaller, than the point is a positive match. In order to compute the threshold, one has be able to obtain the "worst outsider". In other words one has to compute 3.12:

$$Threshold = \min(\{F_3(S, I, S_p, I_p)\}) \forall (S, I) \in \text{"outsiders"} \qquad (3.12)$$

The final segmentation step in which the threshold is compared to the current values, is a separate logical step. It is also possible to use different thresholds in different image areas. For example one may use a different threshold in brighter areas. In this case the threshold has to be computed using a subset of "outsiders" belonging to that region.

One may use statistical methods to find out an average for a specific scene type (for example daylight, normal contrast and brightness). Analyzing several daylight scenes the authors obtained good results by using a threshold placed at 30% of the distance between the "outsider" (255) and the "insider" (0).

3.2.7 Use of the H component

If the SI plane is enough to make a separation between the main types of objects encountered in automotive scenes, what is the use of the H component? The H component has a very important role. First of all it gives the segmentation of an object into subobjects based on color. For a car these sub-objects could be the backlights, tyres, painted surfaces, glass, and so on. If we look for a specific object, and we know its composition, then the H component is the key to recognize the object out of other similar areas in the picture. For example if the system that uses the metrics presented here is a highway assistant it makes sense to look for the backlights of a car when trying to validate new objects. The metric gives the raw points and the higher level algorithm can decide fast whether there is a car in the marked region by looking for the backlights.

There are two crucial aspects. One derives from the fact that there is no color information for elements that have a gray footprint in the picture (white and black are included in the term "gray"). This implies that the H values do not reflect some physical property of the scene element, but are rather noises from the acquisition when the saturation is lower than a certain amount. Lack of a unique color for cars is the second aspect. Thus one cannot rely on a specific color to make the segmentation, but has to find out at runtime what one is looking at before making use of the H information.

One useful clue would be the use of position information. If the position information is ignored the segmentation has no chance to separate two cars of the same color, or vegetation from cars and so on. The easiest way to exploit this information is to design the detection algorithm to process the image data in an ordered manner. This could be from the bottom of the picture up, from left to right or some other paths. The best solution was obtained using a combination of these search algorithms in which the expected form of the object was taken into account.

3.2.8 Performance in various illumination conditions

This subsection deals with the results of the segmentation based on SI metrics in various conditions of scene illumination. Nine different situations are presented, starting with an image that goes into saturation (strong, diffuse lightning) and ending with an image that is underexposed (exit of a tunnel). In all examples, next to the original images, the results of the segmentation are presented as well.

The segmentation uses the function F_3 with adaptive coefficients that were computed as described in 3.2.6.

Before the results are presented, one remark has to be made. Due to performance reasons, the SI segmentation was implemented only from and up to 8 pixels distance from the image margins.

Chapter 3

Figure 3.16: Bright image, almost saturated

Figure 3.17: Bright image, lateral shadow

As seen in fig. 3.16 and 3.17 in situations with direct or very bright sunlight, the camera tries to adapt by reducing the color components (going into saturation). In this case the intensity component can be used to distinguish the objects from the background. In the extreme situation the road will saturate to white and the objects will appear very dark. Such situations pose no difficulties to the segmentation algorithm, since the term $(I - I_p)^2$ in 3.6 will more than compensate for the smaller differences in the saturation. In the extreme situation of very dark objects, the saturation will exhibit higher values than expected (see 3.2.1) and therefore the F_3 function will be able to profit from both factors when comparing object pixels out to the ones belonging to the road surface.

In fig. 3.18 is presented a situation in which large shadows are projected on the road. There are shadows generated by the left trees and by the distant bridge. The segmentation algorithm is robust enough to be able to extract the far vehicle out of the background

3.2 Image Segmentation Based on SI Metrics

Figure 3.18: Bright image, with shadows

and still to be able to correctly classify the shadows as irrelevant (or belonging to the road). This is true even for the distant shadow under the bridge, which is for the naked eye identical to the vehicle bottom.

In all these cases (fig. 3.16 to 3.18) the segmentation in areas of the image that are containing the footprint of the vegetation is performing worse than normally expected. This is due to the fact that when going into saturation, the camera is reducing the contrast of the colors. The reduced contrast is affecting the $(S - S_p)^2$ term in 3.6. The whole image is usually brighter. With other words, the term $(I - I_p)^2$ will also suffer from the reduced contrast.

Figure 3.19: Normal brightness

In normal situations like the one presented in fig. 3.19, the vegetation is most of the time extracted as a compact block (trees and darker parts) or not at all (grass at the

Chapter 3

left and the right of the road). Some unexpectedly dark areas of the road may generate singular errors. The vehicles on the road are extracted with well defined contours, the lower part being accurately segmented out of the road and the shadows surrounding it.

Figure 3.20: Normal brightness with close object

In case of cars painted in silver or white, their resemblance to the lane markings makes a low level segmentation approach inevitably fail. The SI segmentation focuses (due to the $(I - I_p)^2$ term) on the bottom of the vehicle. This area contains the tyres, under vehicle shadows and sometimes the lower parts of the suspension or exhaust are visible. These are generating a very dark footprint that makes possible a successful segmentation as it can be seen in fig. 3.21.

Figure 3.21: Reduced brightness

As the illumination decreases approaching the limits of the normal conditions for the camera the acquisition noise starts to appear. The SI metric based segmentation is directly affected in this case. The reason is the $(S-S_p)^2$ term in 3.6. In case of dark pixels it may or may not exhibit high values, depending one the R,G,B values of the pixel. E.g. for $S_p = 0, I_p = 0$ the point $(R,G,B) = (0,3,0)$ yields $(S-S_p)^2 + (I-I_p)^2 = 255^2 + 1^2 = 65026$. Suppose that the point has now the values $(R,G,B) = (3,3,3)$. Then $F_3 = (S-S_p)^2 + (I-I_p)^2 = 0^2 + 3^2 = 9$. This behaviour is usually triggered by acquisition noises, where some of the pixels are very dark, some exhibit singular noises in one or two of the R,G,B components.

In fig. 3.21, this effect is slightly visible on the segmentation of the vegetation the left side and on the close car on the right side. As the illumination decreases the effect becomes obvious (for example in fig. 3.22 and 3.23).

Figure 3.22: Low brightness image

Figure 3.23: Low brightness image, truck

The images in fig. 3.22 and 3.23 show the performance of the segmentation in the

Chapter 3

case of low illumination. The road surface and the vegetation are dark. They limit the classification possibilities of the $(I - I_p)^2$ term. There are acquisition noises that are affecting the $(S - S_p)^2$ term. The segmentation algorithm produces significantly more singular errors that are visible as "wholes" in the normally compact areas that are marked on the image. Even more, some of the road pixels are so dark, that are able to generate singular segmentation errors due to the $(S - S_p)^2$ term in 3.6.

The segmentation algorithm is still able to correctly separate the vehicles from the background in the presented cases.

Figure 3.24: Underexposed image

The last of the examples presents also an image taken in very low illumination conditions. In this case the SI segmentation is unable to distinguish the vehicle anymore out of the background. The reason is the underexposed image, which makes both background and the car in front of the ego vehicle so dark that they have the same footprint in the image. In this case both terms (saturation and intensity) cannot segment the image properly. If the saturation of the image would have got usable values (like the case of the braking lights), then the segmentation could have been successful.

Summing up, the segmentation based on SI metrics works in most illumination conditions (the notable exceptions are night/extremely dark scenes). There are almost no performance penalties in case of bright scenes. The lower the brightness, the more granular become the segmentation results. They remain usable even for dark scenes as long as the objects are distinguishable from the background. Due to the additional saturation term, the segmentation has more success chances compared to algorithms that are treating image components separately (for example linear color thresholding).

3.2.9 Comparison with other segmentation algorithms

The image segmentation based on SI metrics is not using any position information when sorting the pixels into classes. Therefore it is directly comparable with the linear color

3.2 Image Segmentation Based on SI Metrics

thresholding, nearest-neighbour classification, color space thresholding and probabilistic methods that do not require the position of the pixels in the image during the segmentation. In what follows, the four methods are shortly described. For a more detailed reference, please consult 2.5.3 and the references in the text.

Linear color thresholding works by partitioning the color space within linear boundaries (e.g. planes in 3 dimensional spaces). A particular pixel is then classified according to which partition it lies in. This method is convenient for learning systems such as neural networks, or multivariate decision trees [10].

In nearest-neighbour classification preclassified exemplars are employed, each having a unique location in the color space and an associated classification. To classify a new pixel, a list of the nearest exemplars is found, then the pixel is classified according to the largest proportion of classifications of the neighbours [13].

Color space thresholding is an extension of the linear color thresholding in the 3D color space. Its best results are often obtained when the histogram of the intensity is used to fill in thresholds used in the process. [50].

Probabilistic methods store a discretized version of the entire joint probability distribution [92]. To check whether a particular pixel is a member of the color class, its individual color components are used as indices to a multidimensional array. When the location is looked up in the array the returned value indicates probability of membership. This technique enables a modelling of arbitrary distribution volumes and membership can be checked with reasonable efficiency.

We compare with the first two methods (linear color thresholding and nearest-neighbour). Color space thresholding is a generalized version of the linear color thresholding. Since hue information available in typical automotive scenes is not directly related to a certain class (for more details see 3.2.7), this method will deliver similar results to linear color thresholding. Using the discretized version of the entire joint probability distribution makes possible to model the same results that can be obtained with any of the other methods. For example, if the F_3 metric is used for the computation of the probability distribution, then the method delivers the same results as our segmentation based on SI metrics. The memory requirements to store the entire lookup table and the computing resources required to update it, make the last method unsuitable for this direct comparison.

For the linear color thresholding, two classes were defined. One contains at least the road and the lane markings and the second contains everything else (all relevant objects, etc.) Of course, it is possible that the bright objects are classified as belonging to the wrong class, but such problems are common to all methods that rely solely on the color information. The hue information is not relevant for the road, therefore is ignored for the classification. In order to improve the results of the classification the boundaries of the classes were automatically computed using the results of the road and lane detection (for example the minimum road intensity of the analyzed region; see 3.4.2).

For the nearest-neighbour classification the preclassified exemplars were also automatically updated (road, lane marking, object detection algorithms have provided the required values). In order to compensate for situations in which no objects were detected (there-

Chapter 3

fore no exemplars could be provided for the object class), some predefined (manually obtained from images in the sequence) values were also used. The distance to the pre-classified exemplars was computed using the Euclidean metric.

Before the results are presented, one remark has to be made. Due to performance reasons, the SI segmentation was implemented only from and up to 8 pixels distance from the image margins. The other two methods were implemented to process the complete image.

The results from fig. 3.25 to fig. 3.25 are ordered from left to right: original image, color segmentation based on SI metrics using F_3 (marked with yellow), nearest-neighbour (marked with cyan) and linear color thresholding (marked with magenta).

Figure 3.25: Comparison with other segmentation algorithms - low contrast scene

The scene in fig. 3.25 is a low contrast scene. Few observations can be done without looking into detail:

- the linear thresholding is wrongly classifying road pixels as relevant object pixels
- the SI metric and nearest-neighbour have similar results. The SI metric classifies less from the shadow under the closest car as relevant object pixels
- the results of the SI metric are denser in most areas as the one of the nearest-neighbour algorithm

Figure 3.26: Detail comparison - low contrast scene

If the results are investigated into detail as in fig. 3.26, the following supplementary observations can be done:

- the SI metric segmentation provides for the automotive use the best selectivity in the far regions. Sometimes there is a price to pay, for example in this case is the far car on the right side. It is filtered out by the SI segmentation, while the other two algorithms extract relevant pixels in that area
- the linear color thresholding incorrectly classifies many dark points near the lane markings as relevant object points

The comparison in fig. 3.27 shows the behaviour of the algorithms in the case of near objects and shadows. The following observations hold:

3.2 Image Segmentation Based on SI Metrics

Figure 3.27: Comparison with other segmentation algorithms - close scene

- all algorithms are experiencing problem with strong cast shadows
- the linear color segmentation classifies many road and shadowed areas as object relevant pixels. This can be improved using a more constrictive threshold (the one used is obtained from the road detection algorithm and is influenced for example by bright road regions).

Figure 3.28: Comparison with other segmentation algorithms - far objects

In fig. 3.28 is presented the situation in case of far objects. One characteristic of the far objects is that their shadows are not visible in the picture and therefore they are less demanding on the segmentation algorithms. The following observations can be done:
- all algorithms work properly, extracting at least the lower part of the cars
- for the far objects, the algorithm based on SI metric works less satisfying than the other two. In this work its weakness is compensated by a different detection algorithm for the far objects (see 3.5.6)

Figure 3.29: Comparison with other segmentation algorithms - different objects

The last example is presented in fig. 3.29. This image sequence was taken with another camera having a single CCD imager as opposed to the other sequences which were acquired

Chapter 3

using a 3 CCD camera. There are two observations to be done:
 - the nearest-neighbour and the linear color thresholding extract many dark points near the lane markings as relevant object points. In this example, the lane marking on the right is practically doubled by a line of wrongly classified points by the two algorithms
 - due to the fact that there was no direct illumination of the scene, the linear color thresholding has less classification errors in the road regions
 - the linear color thresholding has difficulties in clearly extracting the motorbike driver from the background. The other two algorithms are working fine in this case

Summing up the following conclusions can be drawn based on these examples and others that were investigated for this work, but not presented here:
 - the linear color thresholding is not able to correctly separate between object, shadows and road pixels. It extracts often pixels corresponding to road, shadow and background as significant pixels. Its weakness is easy to link to the way the color space is divided for the classification. Sections using planes generates rectangular structures in the SI plane. Their form is not matching the conical shapes that are characteristic for elements of the automotive scenes (see 3.2.5).
 - nearest-neighbour classification works almost as good as the classification using the SI metric. Since the nearest-neighbour algorithm computes the distance to the preclassified exemplars by using the Euclidian metric, it can be sometimes very similar to the SI metric. If the preclassified exemplars for the irrelevant class are given by the average road, lane marking and sky values then this method is founded on the same basis as the one based on the SI metric. Unfortunately the costs of going over the list with preclassified exemplars for all pixels, make this method significantly slower that the other two.
 - the classification employing the SI metric performs in most automotive scenes better than the other two methods. The weakness that was identified (detection of the far objects) is related to the fact that in those cases the saturation exhibits small values (due to the small quantity of reflected light the camera sensitivity is probably limiting the resolution of the colors) and the intensity is defining the object footprint in the picture. Since the F_3 metric used is weighting both saturation and intensity equally, its sensitivity is in these cases almost cut in half. In this work this weakness was compensated by employing another detection algorithm in case of far objects (see 3.5.6). This algorithm is using the intensity information combined with form information to detect these special objects in the picture.

3.3 Top-level View

The lane and object detection algorithms are almost completely isolated. The few data that needs to be exchanged between them is the high level environment information that is used to help the some of the 3D position reconstruction algorithms for objects. This makes possible for the future development to separate the two algorithms and let them run on different hardware devices. The top-level structure was already presented in fig. 5.2. A more detailed diagram of the system is illustrated in fig. 3.30.

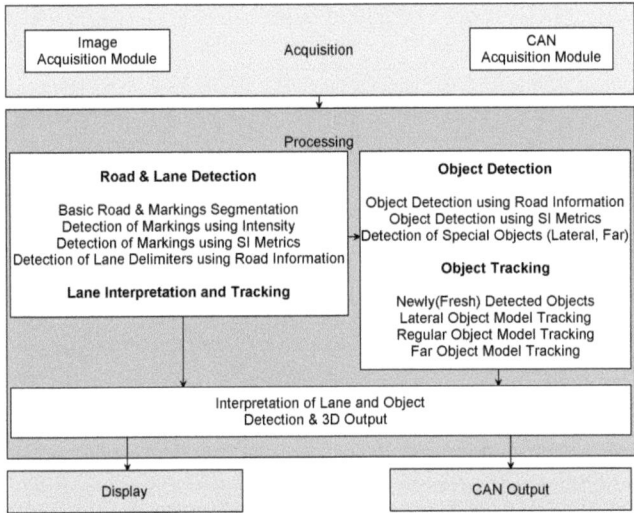

Figure 3.30: CCVS Algorithms - Top-level Structure

The execution starts with the conversion of the Red, Blue, Green (RGB) image into the Hue, Saturation, Intensity (HSI) representation. To be able to keep the realtime requirements, the conversion is implemented as a lookup table with a 24 bit index (a total size of 64Mb).

Next, a basic recognition of environmental (illumination) conditions is done (not illustrated in fig. 3.30). This is just a basic average of the intensity to get a first feedback about day/night conditions.

The lane detection is then performed. There are 3 methods for lane detection:

L1. The first one is to use the known structure of the environment to search for white regions that may be lane markings. Out of them the brightest is chosen and the intensity values are then used to complete the segmentation. The resulted areas are grouped using the direction and then interpolated to get the description of the lane

Chapter 3

delimiters. This method works very well for uninterrupted markings. Due to the internal data representation (vertical segments), the method has problems with almost vertical markings, as can be found during a lane change.

L2. The second one is using SI Metrics inside some regions of interest that are dynamically updated. This method was particularly optimized for interrupted (dotted) lane markings and handles actively the case of lane changing by predicting where the new markings will appear and predetecting them.

L3. The last and the simplest method is using the results from the initial road detection (from method L1) to obtain the left and right delimiters of the lane in which the ego vehicle is positioned. These are interpolated to obtain the left and right delimiters. Even if almost trivial, the method has the advantage of being very robust in case of missing lane markings, when the lane is delimited by grass or other surfaces.

The first method may theoretically deliver up to 8 lane delimiters (in practice, if present, 4 to 5 delimiters are detected), the second up to 3 and the last one a maximum of 2. This makes the fusion of the results not trivial, given the fact that the methods may also fail and deliver wrong results. A special fusion of the results is then performed. During this fusion a minimal conversion to metric 3D coordinates is performed in order to validate the results.

The object detection starts after that. Since the objects are more complex and harder to interpret than the lane markings, a multi-model approach is performed. There is an object detection step in which the objects are detected. There are 4 methods of detecting objects:

OD1. Object detection based on SI segmentation. This is the most important method and is based on image segmentation using SI metrics as described before. In the resulting image, the almost horizontal areas are found and delivered to object tracking. Even if very accurate, the method produces a lot of false positives, especially at the positions where vegetation is to be found.

OD2. Object detection based on road information (from method L1). This is the most basic method. It searches for objects in the ending road regions. It also assumes a horizontal appearance of the bottom of the vehicle in front of us. It produces false positives in the patched road regions or when shadows are present in the image.

OD3. Lateral object detection. The system has a special model to compensate for the lack of form of the vehicles entering the picture. This model uses one region of interest at the left limit and one at the right limit of the image. It watches the changes in intensity in these regions. If they differ significantly from the road average values, than it is supposed that a lateral object is entering/exiting the picture. The regions are created using the information from lane detection and updated dynamically to not override the lane markings.

OD4. Far object detection. It is performed on several image rows, positioned dynamically by previously far object tracking. It is a simple, but effective algorithm. It also delivers false positives. This is not a problem since the tracking is robust enough to reject the ones that are not to be found in the next frames.

The resulted raw objects are described by position information and several other attributes. They are filtered to eliminate the fake positives (not illustrated in fig. 3.30). The filtering is performed with SI metrics that eliminate the vegetation and with a position/size description that is generated dynamically from the already detected objects.

The filtered objects are given to the object tracking algorithms. The object tracking is working with different object models to accommodate the large aspect differences for close and far objects. There are four object models (fresh, normal, lateral and far). The system is defined in such a way that a model can be easily added without changing the software structure.

Finally the object and lane data is converted fully into 3D coordinates and prepared to be outputted on CAN or displayed on the source RGB images. Special attention was paid to the image copy operations which are extremely expensive since the image contains 32 bits per pixel (to speed up the pixel access on current 32 bit architectures, the 32 bit format was preferred to the 24 bit one). The results of the processing are outputted on the CAN bus and on the user screen and the whole cycle is run again. The output is synchronized using a timestamp generated on CAN by the GPS sensor.

Looking at the number of these algorithms, few observations need to be made. It is uncommon for so many different algorithms to be implemented for a single purpose (the best example is the lane detection where 3 algorithms are delivering similar results). The reason beyond this decision was that often a single algorithm may experience problems in special situations. Such cases are typically caught with special handlings.

In this work, the feasibility of a fusion concept using more relatively simple algorithms and merging their results was investigated. Each algorithm for itself is responsible to cover only parts of the complete situation. By merging them, the coverage of the complete situation was tested. In the next sections (see 3.4.7 and 3.5.1) it is shown that this solution often works better than single algorithms and offers a higher possibility of obtaining a performant system. The investigation of how these algorithms can be merged optimally opened another research direction that needs to be followed in the future work that will base on this research topic (see 6.1.2).

3.3.1 Thread Layout

This subsection focuses on the required thread structure that permits the real time performance of the system. The application threads are detailed in fig. 3.31.

In fig. 3.31 each thread is depicted as a blue circular structure with the running order shown as an arrow. The synchronization points are depicted as red rectangles with "x" signs, the position in which one of the threads waits for another is shown as a dotted line that breaks the circle. The synchronization points correspond in the software to setting a single semaphore; the wait positions correspond to either "start - wait - continue" sequences which are controlled using semaphores or to exclusive sections, depending on the particular situation.

The DirectX 9 thread runs outside the application software, in the DirectX library. The thread is built and controlled by the application. It runs a continuous buffered acquisition and delivers the latest acquired image (at a rate of 25 fps, this give an average delay of 20

Chapter 3

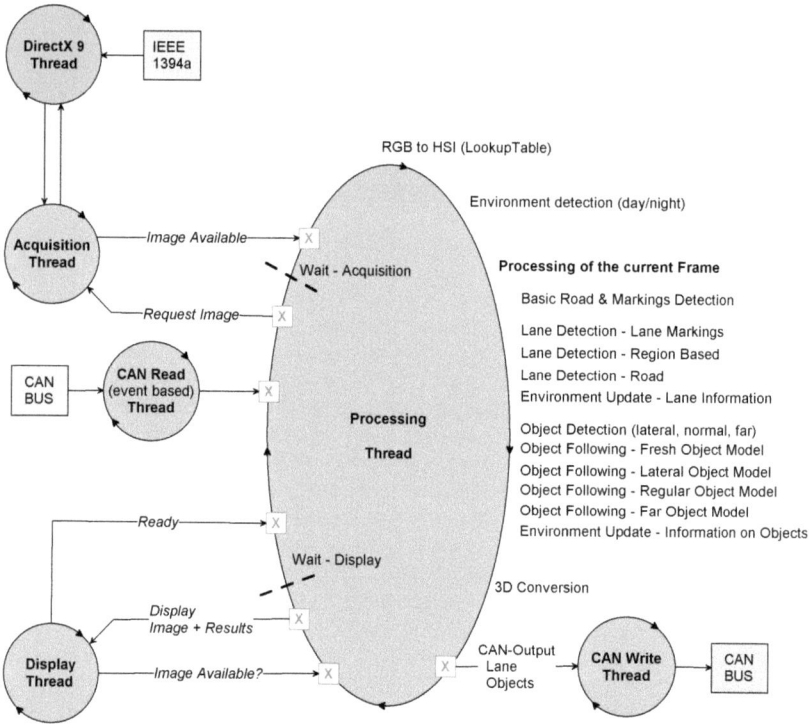

Figure 3.31: CCVS-Online Threaded Structure

ms for the acquisition). The acquisition thread, when invoked, only copies this image to the processing thread, performing simultaneously the required deinterlace and subsample operations.

The acquisition may also run in an independent (not triggered) mode. In non-triggered mode it continuously acquires images and only passes the pointer to the latest image buffer for direct processing. This mode is recommended to be used on very performant architectures with plenty of cache and preferably multiple processors (using this mode gave performance improvements only on an Athlon 64 FX-53 processor; 2 MB of cache, 2,4 GHz; on a P4 1,7 GHz 512 KB the performance loss was about 30% due to processor cache trashing).

The CAN access is performed with two threads. The first is used for reading; it runs independently triggered by the CAN driver (the main thread only checks for available data, without controlling the CAN reading thread). The second is used to output the

3.3 Top-level View

data. It is triggered by the main thread after its data is prepared in the CAN output structures. It marks the data structures as locked, returns the control to the processing thread, writes the data in the background to the CAN driver and releases the lock on the data structures. Since the CAN output takes considerably less that the processing itself, the processing will typically have the CAN output data structures unlocked when needed to write the new data. If this condition is not fulfilled the processing thread will skip the CAN output (as long as CAN output data structures remain locked). This ensures that the data written on the CAN is always the latest available, regardless of the CAN output performance.

The display of the results runs in a specific thread that is the same with the Borland VCL's main thread (thread treating the window messages). In order to be able to conform to the realtime requirements, the output is drawn using OpenGL, therefore it frees the processor from the drawing operations. The output (display) thread copies the source RGB image from the processing thread directly into OpenGL memory and uses OpenGL functions to draw the results. During the copy of the image and the invocation of OpenGL commands (but not their final output which happens independently in the graphic card driver), the processing thread has to be paused to avoid overwriting the RGB image in the next acquisition step. Using multiple buffers to avoid the extra copy is not possible due to the architecture of the non-triggered acquisition mode which has its own buffer management.

These application threads were designed in such a way as to avoid processor trashing, while keeping the operations that can be parallelized into separate threads. This design allows maximum efficiency, by ensuring that the processing thread is not paused by time consuming operations like CAN output, display of the source image with the overimposed results, interaction with the user using the GUI, etc.

This threaded architecture has the disadvantage that debugging is very hard. To compensate, a linear architecture was used for the debug application. It uses the same code, but the scheduling is completely rewritten to be single-threaded and linear. This separation between the two applications allows an optimal debugging and development environment while not sacrificing performance from the online application.

Chapter 3

3.4 Road & Lane Detection

The automotive environment has its particularities, materialized in both the elements that may appear in a scene and their aspect. These particularities can be used not only to speed up the processing, but they can be gathered together in order to form a minimal knowledge base on which the algorithms can be designed or can be dynamically updated.

In other words, the aim is to generate an interpretation of the acquired scene based on apriori knowledge (linked to the specific environment) and on knowledge generated at runtime (linked to the specific system input). We call the first type of knowledge "implicit assumptions" and the second type "inferred assumptions". The next subsection sums up the knowledge used for the detection of the road and of the lane markings.

3.4.1 Knowledge given by the Automotive Environment

The implicit assumptions are in case of road/lane markings:

a) The road is the first visible area in the lower part of the image starting from an arbitrary offset (to avoid problems due to the visible car hood at the bottom of the image). There cannot be an implicit assumption about the presence or absence of lane markings in the lower part of the image. The algorithm has to cope automatically with the presence of lane markings in the area when estimating the average values for the road.

b) Lane markings are present on the road and thus, we can detect the lane markings by scanning the image areas situated near the road regions.

c) Lane markings have a "smooth" direction. A dashed lane marking part starts in the same direction that the previous part ended and not randomly in the picture. This assumption is used when grouping together the detected markings.

d) Lane markings do have special characteristics (bright areas, small inner intensity variation, limited width, same width for one marking). These are discussed in detail in the section dedicated to the lane markings detection.

The inferred assumptions are related to the average values of the hue, saturation and intensity components for the road and lane markings. The algorithms use these values for the segmentation of the image into road and non-road areas as well as for the extraction of lane markings. Since these values vary significantly with the illumination of the scene and the setup of the camera, they are unsuitable as implicit assumptions and must be recomputed over and over again for each acquired image. No sequence information is used for the road and lane markings detection, but the information gathered from the processing of prior images is used to enforce the computed average values. This allows the filtering of outliers and improves the stability of the computed average values.

3.4.2 Road Detection based on Intensity and Saturation

A sketch of the system structure is illustrated in fig. 3.32. There are four distinct algorithm steps. The first three of them (road pre-detection, lane marking pre-detection and finally road detection) are presented in this subsection. The last one, even if using the

3.4 Road & Lane Detection

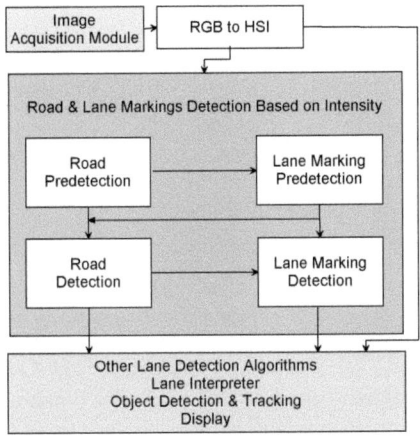

Figure 3.32: Diagram of the system

same underlying methods and data is presented separately in the lane marking detection section where it belongs semantically.

Road Pre-Detection

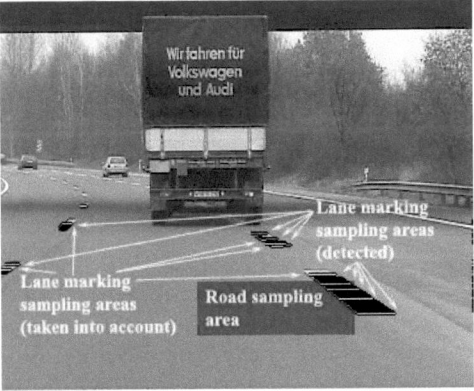

Figure 3.33: Road and lane markings sampling areas

The road pre-detection starts by analyzing a small region at the bottom of the picture to find out the average values of Hue (H), Saturation (S) and Intensity (I) for the visible road

Chapter 3

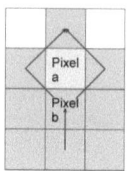

Figure 3.34: Vertical Fill Algorithm

area in the picture (as presented in fig. 3.33). The bright regions are eliminated from this area (most likely they are lane markings) and the rest of the values are averaged to produce the thresholds that are used to limit the search of the road. Since the H component has no meaning for gray objects, only the S and I components are used in all algorithms dealing with road or white lane markings. Hue is used only when looking for yellow lane markings or when validating shadows (usually shadows give uniform Hue values compared to cars which are composed of different surfaces).

The road is then detected using a vertical fill algorithm that extends upwards until it hits a discontinuity in one of the SI components. The algorithm is presented briefly in fig. 3.34. It presents the two successful cases in which the algorithm includes the current pixel in the result. In the first case the algorithm deals with pixel a (second row from bottom, middle pixel) that has values of S and I close enough to the averages given as input parameters and includes it directly. In the second case it encounters a discontinuity in the S or I values for the pixel b (third row from bottom, middle; the darker, red pixel). Since this discontinuity may be a local noise (e.g. salt and pepper noise) the algorithm tries to go over it by checking the nearby columns. If at least one of the two values (left, right) are in the allowed range for S and I and no point of edge is present in that specific location, the algorithm goes further. If not, the search is aborted and the position of the discontinuity is returned.

Two issues are addressed by the design of the algorithm. As most of the methods based on color similarity this particular algorithm has to deal with the problem of local discontinuities (edges) and global discontinuities (going over a range of pixels that are slowly changing between two different surfaces). The local discontinuities are solved in the manner described above. The best results were encountered if the local value was taken into account for the computation of the average values for the next step of the algorithm. In order to provide robustness to noises, the new averages are computed as a weighted average where they have a 5% weight. To solve the global discontinuity problem the algorithm makes an extra check with the initial averages.

The results of applying the fill algorithm are presented in fig. 3.35).

The detected vertical limits for the road are passed on to the lane pre-detection algorithm. The next section discusses possible failures that may occur when estimating the average parameters.

3.4 Road & Lane Detection

Lane Pre-Detection

The lane pre-detection algorithm receives the vertical limits from the road pre-detection. It estimates the average I values of the nearby regions that are brighter than the road surface. These regions are found by using the same sort of vertical fill algorithm but with those values that caused it to stop in the previous step as input. These areas might correspond to possible markings or objects on the road. It is likely that lane markings have the brightest footprint in the picture compared to other objects on the road (cars). Based on this assumption the algorithm selects the brightest regions out of those and computes the average SI values for the markings which will be used later in the lane markings and road detection algorithms. In fig. 3.35 the brightest regions were drawn using white lines surrounded by black areas, the others with a darker color.

If the road sample contains image information of a near vehicle, the correct road SI values cannot be reliably computed; i.e. the computed values will have nothing in common with the actual average SI values for the road surface. The algorithm overcomes these problems by checking the frame average SI values against the sequence averages. This guarantees that singular errors are filtered out. In order to avoid the selection of an area belonging to a car at start-up (when starting the system there are no average values for the sequence) the singular error filtering condition is relaxed for the first 300 frames.

Road Detection

The input for the algorithm consists of the limits of the road (interrupted by any discontinuity, lane markings included) and the average values that were computed in the previous phases. Additionally, the assumptions mentioned in 3.4.1 are used as additional clues when the SI averages are not sufficient to limit the search. The algorithm continues to extend the road limits in the same manner as for the pre-detection phase until they hit something that cannot be categorized as a lane marking or a shadow. That is, every time the search is aborted due to a discontinuity, the algorithm checks the SI values of the point of discontinuity against the averages extracted as characteristic for the lane marking in the lane pre-detection phase. If the deviation of the values is greater than a chosen threshold (relative value) the search is stopped. The handling of shadows is described in the next paragraph. This way all columns belonging to road regions (the columns may contain lane markings inside) are extracted.

Moreover, there are road regions that are not uniform (they consist of several different surfaces; either due to reparations or different construction materials). Fortunately, most of them are similar to shadows in the way they influence the image components. All of them are darker or brighter areas having a small inner variation and gray-scale aspect. The algorithm overcomes these difficulties (hard to solve by comparison with the HSI average values) by adding an extra check for the uniformity of the SI values inside the area above the discontinuity in the vertically oriented fill algorithm.

Two extra constraints were added in order to avoid the algorithm becoming too greedy to label regions that do not belong to the street as road when the image contrast is low. First, the maximum number of discontinuities on a specific image column is limited to 4.

Chapter 3

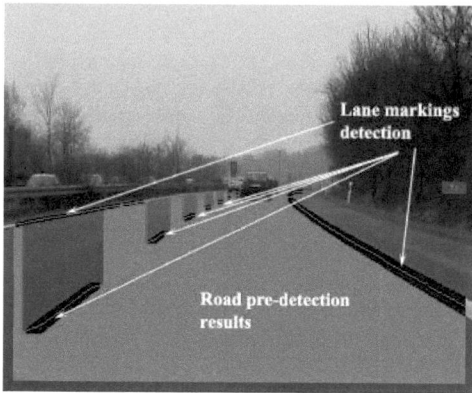

Figure 3.35: A typical road image with the road pre-detection and lane markings detection results drawn on the picture

This affects negatively the completeness of the detection results when there are a lot of small shadows on the road, but avoids detection running into vegetation or sky if they look similar to road. Second, the results of the edge detection are taken into account when trying to pass over a discontinuity in the SI space by using the nearby columns. If an edge point is found in the vicinity of an SI discontinuity the search is aborted.

A situation that is not completely solved by this approach is encountered during sunrise or sunset. Some areas of the distant road shine into the image, while the close by areas look darker. If these areas are not large enough they cannot be classified as shadows/patches and they will be missed. During night time the acquisition signal/noise ratio is smaller and the road pre-detection algorithm terminates too early due to the big number of discontinuities caused by noises. Usually the road detection algorithm hits the first lane markings and the lane marking detection will extract the marking (by extending it), but the results are usually unstable. Both cases require a special handling apart from the algorithms described here.

The output of this step consists of a number of vertical segments for each column. This is what is drawn in fig. 3.36 as the road detection result.

Handling Shadows

Another often encountered aspect for all road and lane marking detection algorithms is related to shadows. Shadows generate extraneous regions which sometimes are hard to identify and therefore generate a lot of noise in the result set. Color is a largely accepted solution in this case, see for example [35] or [94].

Sometimes, due to the camera behaviour or to the road spectral response, shadows cannot be recognized using only intensity information. Hue, saturation and variation of

3.4 Road & Lane Detection

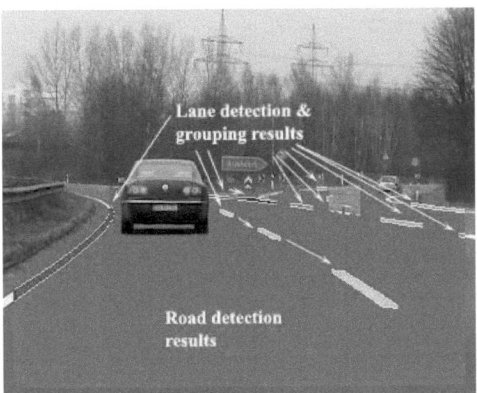

Figure 3.36: Lane markings and road detection results; lane markings are grouped (one color is used per group)

the HSI values inside the area are to be used as well. The weight of the hue component is minimal because of its non-determination in gray pixels. Some authors state that shadows only modify the intensity parameter. This is particularly true when the analyzed region has a well defined color (e.g. green). Since the road does not usually have a true color (gray can be any color with a sufficiently low saturation) and the imaging sensors have limited accuracy it results in practice that shadows induce significant changes in all three HSI values.

Our solution identifies a discontinuity as shadow if
- the region above in the picture has small variations in all HSI values
- after it ended, road specific intensity values were found.

In other words we used the assumption that a shadow was situated on the road and that it was uniform in intensity. This approach proved to be robust enough to cope with all common situations on highway and country roads, in all illumination conditions.

3.4.3 Cognitive Lane Marking Detection based on Intensity and Saturation

The lane detection is carried out in all regions that are situated near the end of the determined road extents. The lane detection algorithm delivers not only lane segments as separate pieces, but it tries to group all segments that are associated to an interrupted lane marking and deliver the whole marking as a single object. Later on, this helps to overcome tracking problems when the tracked lane marking corresponds to a non continuous marking.

The algorithm exploits the implicit assumption that the lane markings are "bright areas imposed/painted on the road surface" and that "they have small inner intensity variations". Using the same fill algorithm as for road-pre-detection but with the average values computed in the lane pre-detection phase as input parameters, it finds all areas that are close to the previous detected road limits and which do have the expected average S, I values. This leads to the extraction of a series of separated segments that have a starting point and a certain length (vertical segments in the picture). If a region that is close to the road in the picture is not bright enough, it will not be extracted as a part of a lane marking.

Using the assumption that "lane markings cannot exceed certain widths" the rough errors of the detection are filtered out. The segments are checked against the left and right neighbouring segments and if the neighbours have similar lengths, but the original segment is too short or too long, then its width is adjusted to the average of its neighbours.

Taking into account that "lanes have a relatively constant width" and that "lane markings are smooth curves" the algorithm improves the form of lane segments and extends the incompletely determined ones. The form is improved by considering the fact that the lane marking should be wider at the bottom than in the upper part of the picture (distant objects are smaller in the picture). The algorithm requires that each segment is smaller in length than (or equal to) its previous neighbour. Using the same observation, the algorithm tries to extend a detected segment that has no upper neighbour by searching within the image column where the neighbour is missing for an area that has the similar SI value and a smaller or equal length. This particular step helps recovering most of the segments that are not being detected because the road detection algorithm stopped before reaching them.

Using the last assumption ("lane markings are smooth curves") it groups the segments regarding their position in the picture (obtaining what we call "lane parts") and computes for each group a direction in which it tends to point. This direction is represented as a first degree curve ($y = ax + b$) and is computed from the list of middle points of each segment. At this stage the segments are grouped in lane parts based on their position in the picture. Still if the lane marking is a dashed one the grouping of different parts will not succeed since they are separated by road regions in the picture. The computed direction is used to group these parts together by checking if their equations in the image are similar. This is the final output of the lane detection phase: groups of vertical segments that are drawn on the output picture.

3.4.4 Lane Marking Detection based on SI Metrics

Generic Algorithm Description

In order to speed up the processing this algorithm works with regions of interest (ROIs). The regions of interest have a trapezoidal form, being specified by the position and width of the base segments. Each region of interest (ROI) will produce at most one lane marking equation at the end of the processing. The size and position of the ROIs are updated automatically during the processing of the current image data. The algorithm manages the ROIs at runtime using the knowledge about the structure of the environment.

3.4 Road & Lane Detection

The algorithm computes the SI metric values of each image pixel in each ROI. The formula is derived from 3.6, by computing the divider dynamically in each cycle 3.13 and reversing the value scale in order to have the smallest distance as the biggest value of the metric function:

$$M_3 = 255 - max\left(\frac{(S - S_p)^2 + (I - I_p)^2}{Divider}, 255\right) \quad (3.13)$$

Using a dynamically computed threshold, the metric values in each row (the y coordinate) are converted to binary (above the threshold or not). Out of these values the middle of the largest segment of 1's is chosen. This gives the x coordinate of a lane marking point.

The algorithm extracts a list with points (a list of (x, y) pairs) for each region of interest. The x,y pairs in the list are to compute a least square approximation of the equation $a * x + b = y$. These coefficients are passed to the lane interpreter. There is no curvature computation in this algorithm. The curvature computation will occur in the lane interpreter.

Management of the ROIs

(a) Init Phase   (b) Regions Updated

Figure 3.37: Regions of Interests for SI Metric Computation

The ROI management algorithm works closely integrated with the lane interpreter. The lane interpreter has normally at the output 2 equations of the form $a * x + b = y$. These equations are used to compute also the y coordinate of the vanishing point of the scene (the vertical position of their intersection). The equations together with the vanishing point are given to the ROI management algorithm as placement hints. The algorithm looks for any active ROI containing the equation. If it does not find any, it will create a new region. In fig. 3.37(a) such an example is illustrated. The image is the

Chapter 3

first in the sequence (i.e. no ROIs before). Using the data from the lane interpreter the two ROIs are created.

Performing a lane change is a critical moment for all lane detection algorithms. One problem derives from the fact that the mathematical representation in the form $a*x+b = y$ looses its efficiency (a has very large values, in the case when the marking is perfectly vertical, the equation cannot be used anymore in this form). The other problem is that the lane detection itself may be limited to extract only two markings. It could in this case extract randomly the left or right lane delimiters depending on the particular image data. The ROI management predicts when such a situation will happen (the angle of one of the equations of the active ROIs ("vertical ROI") with the vertical axis is smaller than a typical angle, 10 grad was used in the algorithms). If such a situation is detected, then for the closest ROI to the "vertical ROI" a mirrored ROI is created (if it does not already exist). This method is based on the supposition that the two lanes on the left and right side of the "vertical ROI" have very similar widths. In practice this turns out to be true in almost all cases (the few exceptions were encountered in construction areas with lane widths of about 3,5 and 2,5 meters).

A ROI is deleted if it is too short (height smaller than a minimum height constant, currently 30 pixels). This may happen if the ROI is positioned at one of the picture margins. Since the ROI limits cannot exceed both the vanishing point and the limits of the image, the region may be too small and in conclusion will be deleted.

If the ROI has no enough points of the estimation of the equation coefficients in $a*x+b = y$, it will be deleted. This means in practice that fewer than 4 rows in the ROI are containing the minimum of 3 consecutive points in which the metric 3.13 value is bigger than the "Threshold".

If the ROI equation produces an angle bigger as a preset value (60 grads was used) with the vertical axis, the ROI will be deleted.

In each cycle the existing ROIs are updated. The updated values are:

- position and width. The ROI is positioned in such a way that the following requirements are met: (i) the computed a, b equation coefficients apply to the middle of the two trapezes basis and (ii) at each image row, all points in which the metric returned a value bigger than the threshold are included in the ROI. Eventually, two corrections are performed to the width (similar to the most rudimentary tracking): (i) the latest horizontal displacement is added on the side where the displacement was detected, (ii) a small constant (4 pixels) is added to the other side of the ROI.

- height. The height of the ROI is set in such a way that at least 8 rows with useful data (segments corresponding to the bright areas) are extracted. The minimum height of 30 rows is to be respected, even when all 30 deliver valid data. If the last part (top) of the ROI does not deliver useful information, the ROI is extended upwards until one of the following conditions are true: (i) the last 5 rows all contain useful information (ii) the maximum height of 130 pixels is reached. This behaviour was introduced to deal with the interrupted lane markings and proved to be extremely efficient.

- threshold and divider for 3.13. Both are discussed together with the metric in 3.4.4.

3.4 Road & Lane Detection

Specific implementation of the SI Metric

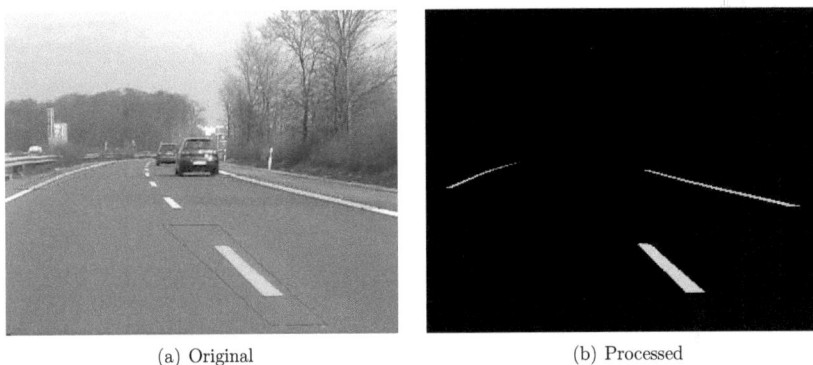

(a) Original (b) Processed

Figure 3.38: Results of applying the SI Metric to the ROIs

The threshold and the divider are computed with the algorithm described in the dedicated subsection 3.2.6. The computation is straight ahead as in the formula 3.11.

The "bad", respectively "good" values are computed as averages of the ROI points in which the metric value is smaller, respectively bigger than the threshold.

The values are initialized as follows: divider = 512, threshold = 230. The reference S,I values (S_p and I_p in 3.13) are set by default to the values returned by the lane predetection algorithm.

Fig. 3.38(a) presents a traffic scene with three ROIs. This is typical for a lane change situation. The green points inside the ROIs are the points exceeding the threshold. One may see in 3.38(b) the result of applying the metric with the dynamically computed coefficients. The contrast is improved, there are almost no noises in the processed image. The situation remains the same in lower contrast scenes or shadows.

The resulted values are then thresholded at each image row in the ROI giving a binary 0,1 list. The longest segment of 1's in the list is chosen and its middle will be used for the interpolation of the a, b coefficients in the equation of the marking $a * x + b = y$. The complete description is presented in the section 3.4.7 when detailing the merging of the results of the lane detection algorithms.

3.4.5 Lane Delimiters Detection based on Road Detection Results

Both of the presented methods until now are limited to situations when the lane markings are present on the road surface. They have also some inertia due to their learning of the average values or metric coefficients. There are situations when no markings are present or when the changes occur so quickly that no adaptation is possible (e.g. when driving in a curve with a small radius with shadows on the road).

Chapter 3

In order to be able to cope with such situations a very simple, not necessarily performant algorithm was required. The purpose was to use its results to speed up the positioning of the ROIs and the computation of average values for the other algorithms. The solution chosen was to use the results from the road predetection, that were already available and to drop all the reasoning about the lane marking properties. The algorithm is therefore outputting lane delimiters (may be also the transition from road to grass for example).

Interpreting the road predetection results

The road predetection algorithm was presented in 3.4.2. The output of the algorithm is a list of vertical positions (one for each horizontal position between 8 and the width of the image - 8) where the road detection was interrupted due to a discontinuity in the I and S components. In fig. 3.35 the results are graphically illustrated. These points are the input of the lane delimiters detection algorithm; in what follows they will be referred to as the source points. In order not to affect other algorithms using the same vector as input, a local copy is created.

The road predetection algorithm can theoretically return more than 2 markings. When the optical axis of the camera is close to the middle axis of the vehicle, the most of the points will belong to the interruptions at the limits of the traffic lane in which the ego vehicle is driving.

The notion of "boundary" is encountered in the description of the algorithm. A boundary is a set of points out of the "source points". The algorithm starts by selecting the point with the lowest vertical position (closest to the bottom of the picture). A new boundary containing the point is created. For each point in the set, the algorithm tries to add the point to the new boundary. The point is added if its distance in image coordinates is less than 8 pixels (empirically found). That means that a point placed at 5 pixels distance vertical and 5 horizontal will the most distant that will be added. If the point is added, then remove it from the "source points". After processing all points the algorithm starts over from the beginning by creating a new boundary until no element is left in the "source points".

In the last step of the algorithm, the points of each boundary are interpolated to generate an equation of the form $a * x + b = y$. These equations are fed into the lane interpreter. The results are also illustrated in fig. 3.39. In this figure both the ideal case for the algorithm (the lane marking on the right) and the worst case (the road patch in the middle) are present. The algorithm itself being very simple, it lacks the analysis capabilities of the other algorithms. But at the same time, this turns out to be a tremendous advantage in relatively unstructured environments or in quick changing scenes. Since the algorithm has no history (it is a "single frame" algorithm) it is used mostly in the preliminary phase of the other algorithms to provide basic information that can be used for a quick start-up. The results are only integrated by the lane interpreter if no reliable results are delivered from the other two algorithms.

3.4 Road & Lane Detection

Figure 3.39: Lane Boundary Detection based on Road Predetection Results

3.4.6 Yellow Lane Markings

Construction areas on public roads are a permanent source of traffic problems. The special marking of these areas, the reduced width of the lanes and mostly the high quantity of older information (lane markings, traffic signs) without semantics raise problems that are not present elsewhere.

For a driver assistance system one important aspect is to be able to distinguish between important and meaningless information in such an area.

Most of European countries use yellow lane makings that are over imposed on the existing white lane markings in construction areas. Such conditions do not make a gray-level based approach very useful since both yellow and white colors will convert to relatively high intensity values. This makes a reliable distinction between them difficult if not impossible. In such situations, a common approach is to signal to the driver that an unknown situation was encountered and to suspend the processing waiting for better environmental conditions. Since this work approaches the problem of yellow markings from the point of view of color vision, it has the chance to try to solve the problem of yellow markings as well.

Extending the Knowledge Base for Yellow Markings

During the research related to yellow marking recognition it was quickly found that the knowledge base used in the process of road and lane recognition has to be extended.

Inconsistent lane markings (white markings that are in the right place may or may not be replaced by yellow markings), lack of markings (yellow markings may not be applied at exterior of the road) or incomplete markings are only a few cases which show the complexity of the driving environment in such construction areas.

Chapter 3

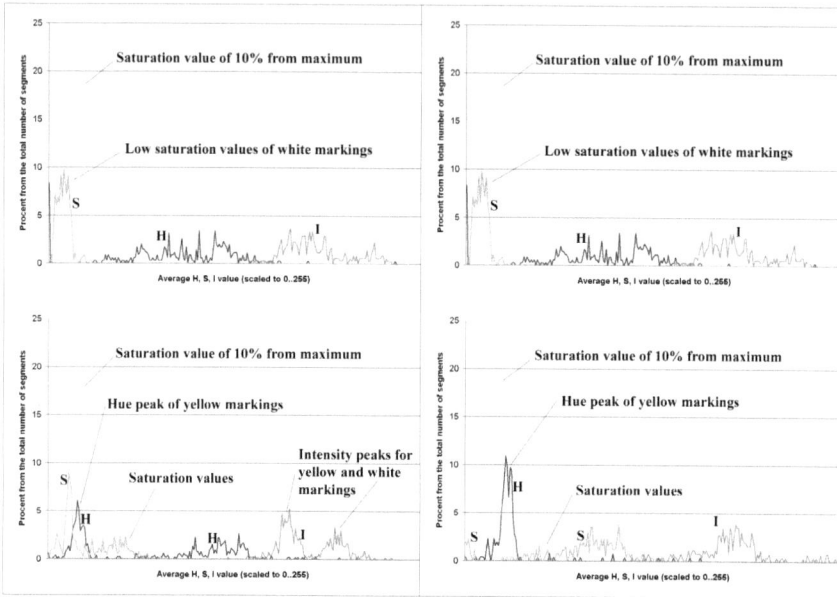

Figure 3.40: Histogram of H, S, I components in the detected lane marking areas at day (left) and night (right). Up: only white markings. Down: both yellow and white markings

The additional assumptions that became part of the knowledge used to deal with yellow markings are listed below:

1) A yellow marking is applied between two traffic lanes (the most common situation). Situations in which yellow markings are on the side of the road and a white marking is present in the middle cannot be treated without using information about the lane size (i.e. a calibrated system which is beyond the scope of this paper).

2) The outer white markings (at the left and right sides of the road) can be valid even if there are yellow markings on the street. If there are yellow markings located close to them the white markings should be dropped out of the processing.

Color Features of the Yellow Lane Markings

An analysis of the three components (H,S,I) is conducted in order to decide what criteria can be used to separate the white markings from the yellow ones. In fig. 3.40 two specific situations are presented. The two histograms on the left column have been obtained from data taken at daytime before and within construction area. The histograms on the right column have been obtained from data taken at night. In order to plot all three components (H, S, I) on the same histogram, a remapping of the respective domains was done to the interval 0..255. Each of the components is analyzed below with its specific advantages and disadvantages:

Hue: In practice the values for the yellow colors associated with the markings depend on the hardware and software setup. Nevertheless they can be generally distinguishable from the values associated with the white markings. In the two histograms at the bottom the presence of a peak for hue components near the beginning of the hue interval can be observed. In our experiments the value given by the camera was close to orange. In all cases in which the yellow lanes are not present the hue component for white mostly consists of noisy values. In the HSI representation white should be represented as having $S = 0$ and accordingly, the H component should then be invalid. It is not always possible to invalidate hue using the saturation information given by the RGB to HSI conversion because of the inherent acquisition noises (the color camera gives no real greyscale values - i.e. having S=0 - but some values in which S is small, still not negligible). Such H values proved to have little influence on the algorithm. The chosen solution was to use the H values without accounting for the saturation. In the lower histograms in fig. 3.40 the peak that characterizes the yellow markings can be distinguished. Its raw value may not always be high enough to count alone as a criteria for distinguishing between the markings, still hue is a valuable piece of information.

Saturation: Comparing the lower histograms with the upper ones it becomes clear that saturation values that are above some specific threshold (this was empirically found to be about 10% from the maximum of the saturation) are observed only if there are yellow markings. The yellow markings give a footprint between 15% and 70% of the maximum saturation. In some particular cases this criterion is still too weak. When the yellow markings are shining due to strong sunlight the footprint tends to be close to 15% and the white areas are somewhere below 10%.

Depending on the light and the camera setup yellow and white markings result in very close intensity levels in the picture. Taking into account the noise of the acquisition it is almost impossible to distinguish between the two intensity levels in almost all cases. An exception can be seen in the lower-left histogram. In this case yellow markings that are not highly reflective generate a second group of lower intensity values on the histogram. Since this information is not always accurate the intensity information is not used at all in this approach.

Detecting the Yellow Markings

The system starts by building the histograms for hue and saturation. It computes the number of saturation values bigger than 15% of the maximum value. If the number is significant the yellow flag is set. If the saturation data lies too close to the threshold then hue is analyzed as well. If no significant percent of values was between dark orange and yellow, then the algorithm concludes that there are no yellow markings present. If yellow markings are found, the algorithm runs further and marks the white lanes as not trusted (based on their hue and saturation average values). At early stages of the development

Chapter 3

direct labelling in yellow and white lanes was tried out without the evaluation of the presence or absence of the yellow markings; it produced very noisy results and even fake yellow markings when the markings did not have a very good footprint in the picture. Since singular values are not accurate enough, this approach focused on evaluating values from all lane markings present in the picture.

If the lane markings detector did not detect enough yellow markings (for example the markings are not continuous or they are old) the above mentioned algorithm has not enough data and is not able to perform well. In such cases a more sensitive but still accurate measure for the presence of yellow markings in the picture is needed. The function should be able to recognize a yellow lane marking that is not expected to be long or to have a strong footprint in the picture. Since it is meant to complement the other method, it was designed to work well especially in cases where the other one fails (when the major part of detected markings is white). The chosen function is based on the weighted deviation of the lane marking H and S values from the average values for all lanes. This function performs very well if the number of segments belonging to yellow markings is less than 10% of the number of total segments. In these cases the saturation and hue of the yellow marking are experiencing a significant deviation from the averages. After an extra check that the lane marking color is close to yellow the algorithm concludes that the lane marking is yellow and the detection was not accurate enough.

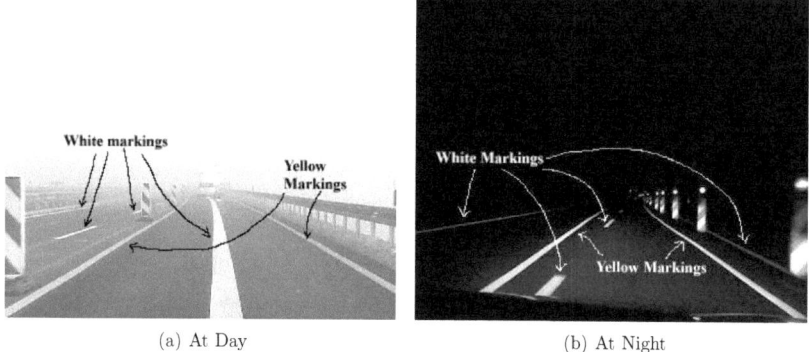

(a) At Day   (b) At Night

Figure 3.41: Typical yellow markings in construction areas

One common situation that occurs in construction areas is illustrated in fig. 3.41(b). The yellow markings are applied on the center and right sides of the road, but no marking is applied over the old white marking on the left. In such situations ignoring all white markings found in the picture means eliminating really valuable information. There are no criteria based on color that enable the distinction between the invalid white markings and the valid ones. The only clue here is the position with respect to the yellow markings. Two approaches are presented here.

The first one uses the results of the road detection algorithm. This algorithm (referred later to as "Position on road") returns the image coordinates where the road extends. Typically, these are the same as the last left or right marking. Accordingly, the first algorithm relies on computing the offset between these extents and the position on which the white lane markings that were already marked as invalid by the color separation algorithm so far. If the result was negative (the lane marking started above the highest limits of the road) than the lane marking was considered valid. There are also cases in which such an approach is inefficient. The situation in fig. 3.41(b) is such an example. The outer right white marking is not valid since its semantics are overridden by the traffic indicators.

The second algorithm can only be used in situations where at least 2 yellow lane markings were detected. It works by estimating the average distance between these markings as a first degree function $dx = ay + b$, where dx is the relative distance in the picture (in pixels) and y is the vertical picture position. Using this template distance it checks the distance to the closest yellow marking for all white markings. The difference is then compared to 40% of the minimum distance of the yellow markings at that Y position in the picture. If it is smaller, then the white marking is dropped. If not, it checks whether the white marking is surrounded by yellow markings. If it is surrounded, then it is dropped. This approach avoids leaving detected white markings that were in the middle of the lane (see fig. 3.41(a)) as valid in the output set.

The connection between algorithms is described below. The "yellow/white separation" algorithm refers to the algorithm for the global analysis of the lane markings; "sense yellow marking" algorithm is the algorithm used for a deeper analysis of the cases in which the lane detection delivered minimal results.

The "yellow markings present" flag is obtained from the "yellow/white separation algorithm". If it is false, the "yellow sense algorithm" is run to enforce the conclusion. The flag indicating poor detection quality is set by default to false and will only be set to true if "yellow sense algorithm" ran and concluded that there was at least one yellow lane marking.

In fig. 3.42 the activity diagram of the system is presented. It works as follows: first of all, the source lane markings are checked one by one by the "yellow/white separation algorithm". The algorithm marks all markings that have low saturation and non-yellow hue averages as not trusted. The "Position on road algorithm" will then restore the trust for those lanes that are the lateral limits of the detected road surface. From these lane markings the ones that are close to the yellow ones will be invalidated by the "Relative position algorithm". This is the final data that is handed over to the Lane Interpreter.

3.4.7 Merging the results - The Lane Interpreter

The on going research in the field showed that each single solution is predestined to fail in some particular situation. The main reasons are the variability of the environment and the extreme lightning conditions. Accordingly, this thesis focused on providing multiple solutions for problems like lane marking or object detection. All these solutions have

Chapter 3

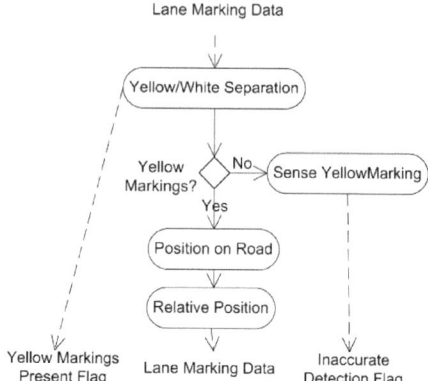

Figure 3.42: Yellow Marking Detection Algorithm

their shortcomings. To simply mix their results using something like an average would bring no better results. Therefore, the solution adopted here was to analyse the output of the methods, even ignoring results that were unexpected and that could not be proved. At the very end an interpretation of the results in the picture was performed as a validation step. Because of this re-validation step, this software module was called the "lane interpreter". This interpreter goes as far as disabling or enabling certain methods and providing hints for quicker start-up phase. It acts like a central coordinator of the lane detection algorithms.

Each of the methods presented until now deliver the results in form of $a*x + b = y$ equations. These equations carry no curvature information. The curvature information is obtained by the lane interpreter when projecting the equations back in the image.

In fig. 3.43 is presented the basic structure of the lane interpreter. The first step is to convert all data to a common representation. The information is then merged and the result is projected back into the source image. The detection results are corrected and the curvature information is extracted. Using the information obtained during the correction, the lane interpreter controls the detection algorithms. For example: if the ego vehicle is driving on a three lane highway in the middle lane (therefore only dotted markings delimitating the lane left and right), then the first detection algorithm (cognitive lane detection) is turned off because its performance is limited by the lower number of points belonging to the markings.

Merging the lane detection results

The first step consists of expressing all detection results in a common format that may be later used for the merge. This format includes in the current implementation the following attributes:

3.4 Road & Lane Detection

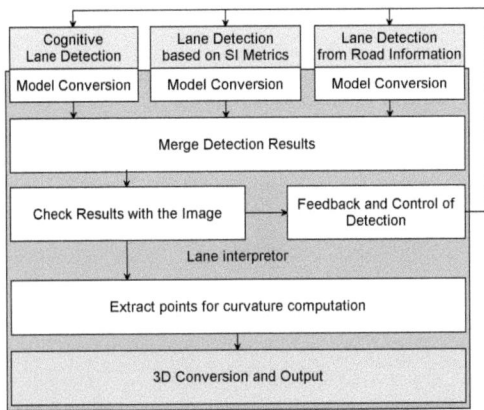

Figure 3.43: Structure of the Lane Interpreter

- the a,b parameter of the equation $a*x+b=y$
- the color of the marking (white, yellow, unknown)
- the type of the marking (continuous, interrupted)
- the status of the marking (newly detected, tracked and verified in the picture, tracked with no picture match, not available)
- the trust of the marking (from 0 to 255, where 0 means not trusted, 255 means absolute trust)
- the valid flag
- the parameters of the clothoid equation (for future extensions, currently no algorithm delivers the information in the form of a clothoid)

Certainly, not all algorithms can fill in all these values. Therefore the lane interpreter has to make informed decisions about which values should be included and which not. Since the final output required only the definition of the ego lane (that is two markings, one at the left, one at the right), only two markings are selected for each detection algorithm. The selection is done by analysing which of the markings is nearer to the known projection of the ego axis on the image bottom.

The algorithm starts by comparing the results of lane detection based on SI metrics (L2) with the results of the detection based on road predetection (L3). Because this particular detection method has no tracking, its results may be the most accurate ones. If the results match up to an arbitrary deviation, than L3 results are taken as reference. If not, the reference is chosen from the first valid results from of the L2 and L1 (detection based on cognitive information about the environment).

Each detection algorithm that does not exceed the arbitrary deviation is then included in the sum used to average the results. This approach has two advantages:
- the most dynamic algorithm has priority if its results are matching the expected

89

Chapter 3

tracked results from L2.
- since no weighting of the detection results can be performed due to the lack of accurate trust information, the algorithm performance of the algorithms (L2, L1, L3) offers the chance to be used instead of the trust information. This gives the interpreter the ability to filter out the singular noises from the remaining algorithms. There is no direct contribution of the tracking of the previous results to the output. For this reason the system is extremely dynamic. This was an advantage when the output was used in a sensor fusion environment based on Kalman filtering.

Comparison of the lane tracker results to single algorithm results

In order to understand the effectiveness of the used approach (to merge results of more algorithms that have their strengths in distinct situations) we present a statistical comparison. The data is gathered from a 2 lane highway scene. The ego vehicle drives most of the time on the right lane. The analyzed data is obtained out of 5000 frames (about 200 seconds) from the whole sequence.

The results are presented in next table (table 3.4.7). The numbers represent the count of the left/right valid flag (maximum 5000) that was outputted by each of the algorithms (each algorithm outputs a valid flag if it has available data for the corresponding lane delimiter). In parenthesis the percent (compared to the 5000 frames = 100%).

Algorithm	Left Delimiter	Right Delimiter
lane interpreter	4349 (86.98%)	4986 (99.72%)
lane detection based on road detection	2002 (40.04%)	2641 (52.82%)
lane detection based on SI metrics	1630 (32.60%)	3178 (63.56%)
lane detection based on intensity and saturation	2908 (58.16%)	4392 (87.84%)

The results of the lane interpreter are outputted for more than 86% (left lane delimiter) and 99% (right lane delimiter) of all frames. The algorithm that has most of the data to present to the lane interpreter is the cognitive lane detection based on intensity and saturation. It reaches a percent of about 66% (left lane delimiter), respectively about 87% (right lane delimiter).

Not taking into account the improvement in the quality of the results, the lane interpreter is able to improve the result with about 28% (for the left delimiter), respectively about 11% (for the right delimiter) in the test scene. This proves the effectiveness of the approach.

Lane curvature and output

After the matching is concluded, there are two equations of the form $a*x + b = y$. These equations are projected on the image. Starting at the lowest position (closest to the image bottom) for each equation an intensity profile in the form of a lane marking is searched.

3.4 Road & Lane Detection

This profile is then interpreted to extract a list of points that are positioned in the center of the profile. The longest list of points is chosen for the computation of the curvature.

These points are used to interpolate the coefficients of a 2D curve of the form $a_0 * \frac{1}{Y_{ri}^2} + a_1 * \frac{1}{Y_{ri}} + a_2 * Y_{ri} + a_3 = X_{ri}$. The indices "ri", show that the position is relative to the optical center and not to the image coordinate system. These coefficients are then used to compute the curvature with the help of the formulas 4.10. The complete description of the 3D reconstruction method is detailed in 4.4. The reconstruction of the other 3D information (lane width, ego displacement) is also treated in 4.4.

The lane interpreter is the final step in the lane detection algorithms. It merges the detection results from more detection sources, tries to compensate their shortcomings and controls the algorithms in order to improve both the running time of the system and the algorithm performance.

Chapter 3

3.5 Object Detection & Tracking

Almost all elements of the road transportation infrastructure that can be used for lane detection (markings, street) are monochromatic elements. Since the amount of color information is extremely reduced, the advantages of using it are also limited. This argument is also confirmed from the fact that lane departure warning systems based on greyscale image processing methods are already in series development at major automobile companies.

On the other hand, this work was dedicated to color vision. It is trying to answer the question "What specific advantages can color information bring to the image processing algorithms in the automotive domain?". Correspondingly, the focus is oriented to object detection where the color information provides a definitive advantage.

The second important direction of this work, the cognitive aspect, was partially highlighted by the road, lane detection as well as by the lane interpreter algorithms. Using simple algorithms and trying to combine the results of the algorithms that perform better in disjunctive conditions to cover the whole application spectrum will be illustrated in all its extent in the object detection algorithms.

The other cognitive aspect, using the knowledge about the automotive environment structure and its properties instead of mathematical models, is less relevant for object detection as for lane detection. The reason for it, is that the objects are harder to define in detail than the traffic lanes. In order to be able to design the algorithms, a minimal knowledge about the form and the properties of the vehicles is required. This topic is presented in detail along with the algorithms using it, but it was considered too small to have its dedicated section.

The major focus of this work is the detection of objects. By object are understood passenger cars and trucks, in order to keep the dimension of this thesis in the imposed timeframe. In order to improve the detection results, the detected objects are tracked between pictures. They are re-detected in each single frame, therefore the output is perfectly suited for a sensor fusion tracking using Kalman filtering.

3.5.1 Multiple Models

Motivation

For any common camera setup (focal length of 500 - 2000 pixels) the size of objects that are present in the picture ranges from almost the width of the picture (in case of a close car in front of the camera) to a few pixels for distances of 200 - 500 meters. Such different footprints in the image suggest that a single object model for detection or tracking will only work in a limited range. Multiple models pose a great challenge to the way they have to be chosen (i.e. an additional recognition step) and bound together. But they are able to cover the complete range required by advanced driver assistance systems.

The system presented in this work not only uses multiple methods to cover the complete visible angle of the camera (up to about 300 meters depending on the sharpness of the image), but a single model uses multiple algorithms to compensate for weak points of a

3.5 Object Detection & Tracking

Figure 3.44: Scene with three different car models (Far, Regular, Lateral)

single method. This structure allows future extensions to the system to be programmed in a natural way, covering failure cases and leaving other functionalities untouched.

Object classes

The objects are divided into three main models (classes) depending on their position in the picture:
- lateral object (partially visible, "touching" one margin of the picture).
- "regular" object (fully visible in the picture, not "touching" any margin of the picture, wider than 24 pixels)
- far object (fully visible in the picture, smaller than 24 pixels)

Each of the main models also has sub-models for passenger cars and trucks.

Fig. (3.44) illustrates the multiple model concept. The red marked object belongs to the lateral model, the yellow one to the regular model and the green one is tracked using a far model. The transition between models is transparent for the output, the new model inherits as much as possible from the old one (position, properties, etc.) and tracks the object without any interruption in the output.

One may also note that the three models are disjunctive; i.e. one object can only belong to a single model. This property is not absolutely necessary if the system would finally perform a union of the results before the output. This study has chosen the simpler method (just an addition of all results of the different models) because there was no need to track a class of objects with two different models. Therefore there is a one to one mapping between object classes and models used for the detection and tracking.

Chapter 3

Overview of the Object Detection and Tracking System

In what follows the raw detected objects in picture will be referred as "candidate objects" (or shortly candidates). Naming detected objects as "candidate" objects is due to the fact that a newly detected object is treated differently in the tracking algorithms as an already tracked object that is changing its tracking model.

Objects redetected using search regions from previous results are referred to as tracked objects or shortly objects. The term "tracked" should not be associated with Kalman filtering. The main reason why the Kalman filtering was not used in this thesis is that the sensor fusion system that integrates this work is already using Kalman filtering. Since the basic assumption in Kalman filtering is that the noises have a Gaussian distribution, using two Kalman filters would greatly diminish the benefits of the second filter.

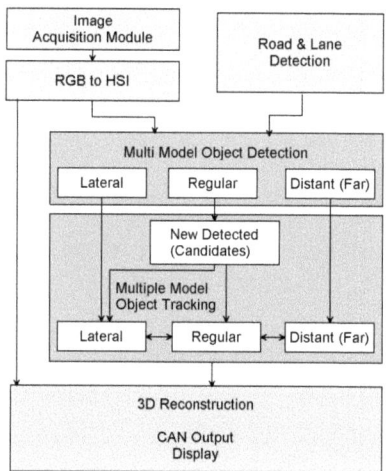

Figure 3.45: Object Detection and Tracking

The object detection and tracking subsystem (see Fig. 3.45) uses information from the road detection, the SI metric segmentation, the lane detection and the source image to generate candidates expressed as rectangles in image coordinates (position, width, height). The candidates are delivered to a specific model that tracks them for the rest of the sequence. No output is generated directly from the candidate detection phase.

After the object tracking block receives the candidates, it performs an association with the already tracked objects. For the remaining candidates, it instantiates objects from one of the models (depending on the properties of the candidate). These instances (tracked objects) will redetect the objects further in the images of the sequence. If during its lifetime an object changes (drives closer or too far away from the ego vehicle) such that its model becomes inadequate, it notifies the system that it requires a different tracking model and the system will try to change its model by instantiating the new model and deleting the old instance. Over the lifecycle of an object its tracking models can be seen as nodes in a state graph, each node knowing its neighbours and suggesting when a state change should occur, but the final decision of changing the state (transition between two models) belongs to the system.

3.5.2 Object Detection - System Structure

The detection of objects is performed based on results from the road detection step and on the raw HSI image. Fig. 3.46 illustrates the structure of the object detection system.

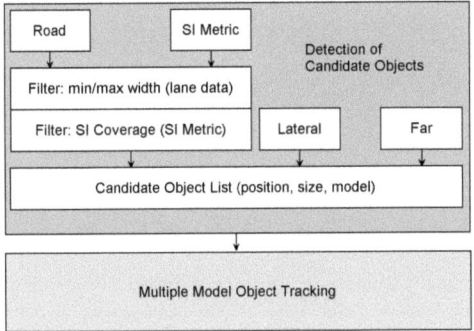

Figure 3.46: Candidate Detection

The objects that are most relevant to a driver assistance system such as ACC, are the objects that are present in the same traffic lane as the ego vehicle, in front of the ego vehicle, hence on a possible collision course with the ego vehicle. Such objects correspond typically to the regular object model. Therefore the object detection focuses on the regular object model. It has two detection algorithms, each with its information source.

The fact that the detection of regular object plays a most important role, is not the same as saying that regular objects are important. If the lateral and distant object detection algorithms would not miss any object, the regular object detection is not necessary at all. An object can only arrive in the range assigned to the regular model if it passes through the other models. But in reality objects may not be detected or it may also be possible that an object is lost during tracking. In such cases, reliable object detection for the regular model is of ultimate importance.

3.5.3 Object Detection - Using SI Metrics

The metric chosen for object detection is the one from (3.6). The same process of updating automatically the coefficients is carried out as for the road and lane marking detection

Chapter 3

algorithm. The reference point for the "good" value is chosen as having I = 0 and S = 128. The reason is the one described in 3.2.1; the S values are high due to the model errors of the HSI representation. The "bad" reference value is given by the average S and I values from the road pre-detection algorithm.

(a) Source Image

(b) SI Metric Results

Figure 3.47: SI Metric Results for Object Detection

The results obtained from applying the metric to the source image are illustrated in fig. 3.47(b). As clearly visible in fig. 3.47(a), the shadows are generating false positives. There is no possibility to eliminate them for the object detection, in the HSI color space, without using higher level information. E.g. the areas inside the shadows have the same HSI values as the areas situated on the vehicle tyres.

Another important observation regards the region of interest for the metric computation. As it can be clearly seen in fig. 3.47(b), the metric is only computed up to a certain vertical position. This avoids computing the metric for about 1/3 of the image points and generates accordingly about 30%-40% speed-up. The exact vertical position is given by the lane detection algorithms in form of the vertical position of the intersection of the two outputted lane delimiters. In order to achieve the required stability, the results are averaged over 50 cycles (about 2 seconds at 25 fps).

The next step in the algorithm is to extract horizontal areas that posses the property that above them all metric values of the points are greater than the threshold (or candidate points as marked on the fig. 3.47(b)) and below them all the points are irrelevant as candidate points. This is equivalent to the fact that the bottom of the footprint of the car (tyres, shadow under the vehicle) is "touching" the road surface, since the road average values were taken as the "bad" reference for the SI metric.

The algorithm implementation is straight ahead. The image rows are parsed one by one and for each row the existence of a region that contains no positive results of the metric but the row only contains positives is proved. The results are of course extremely noisy and include a lot of false positives due to either the lateral vegetation, shadows or

3.5 Object Detection & Tracking

road patches.

Parsing the whole ROI of the metric proved to be inappropriate due to real time constraints. The solution was to limit the results to one match per column. In other words, the criteria had to be: in a single column there is at most one match. This avoided searching the rows further if a candidate was already found at that vertical position. The limitation is not as strict as it may seem. Suppose that no shadows generate false positives on the road. In this case all visible objects are detected, since the closest object to the camera is also the lowest positioned in the picture.

(a) Raw Results   (b) Filtered Results

Figure 3.48: Object Detection Results using the SI Metric

In the next step, these positives are filtered to eliminate the ones that are clearly false positives (using their position and size information). The rest of them will be passed to a specific tracking model, which is parameterized in such a way that it does not promote them to the status of objects ready for output as long as it cannot verify their form and basic properties. The final (filtered) results of the object detection are presented in fig. 3.48(b). The objects detected before the filtering are presented in fig. 3.48(a).

As illustrated in fig. 3.48(b) the filtering may also eliminate distant objects. Since the purpose of this algorithm is not to detect the distant (small) objects, but the near ones, the filtering is complying with its specifications. Moreover, a 100% accurate detection is not a requirement for the reliable functioning of the object tracking. The tracking itself compensates for the objects that were not found during the detection phase.

3.5.4 Object Detection - Using Road Information

The basic idea for the second object detection algorithm remains the same: find horizontal areas in the road detection results. The horizontal areas would probably correspond to objects situated at the end of the detected road areas. The implementation is simplified by the fact that the road detection results are already in the form of an array containing the

Chapter 3

vertical positions where the street ends. The algorithm traverses the road detection results from left to right and looks for horizontal areas (a deviation of 1 pixel is acceptable). If such an area is found, then it is added to the results.

(a) Raw Results (b) Filtered Results

Figure 3.49: Object Detection Results using the Road Detection Results

The road detection results along with the unfiltered objects are presented in fig. 3.49(a). In fig. 3.49(b) is presented the result of filtering the detected objects. As it can be observed, the filtering eliminates all false positives at the road margins. This is done with a filtering algorithm that computes for a detected object (considered as a rectangle) the number of points that are found to be positives by the SI metric. This filtering method is not coupled with the previous algorithm in any way. The filtering is just using the property of the SI metric to clearly separate the road and the marking points from the points belonging to objects.

3.5.5 Object Detection - Lateral Objects

The detection of lateral candidates is treated in detail in [99]. The solution presented in the current article is simpler because the requirements are less strict; to assert the presence and to find the behaviour of the lateral candidate is enough for the purpose of this paper. A complete description in image coordinates in the current implementation is not necessary for the sensor output (since the sensor cannot assert the position of the invisible back of the car, which is the reference point for the sensor fusion model).

Similar to [99] the lateral candidate detection in this paper uses the property that the candidate has to "touch" one margin of the picture. The lane detection gives the limits for the current lane. These limits are used to generate the left and the right lane search regions. These regions are watched for sudden changes in intensity that may indicate that an object "enters" the picture. In order to cope with local noise, areas of 8x8 pixels are averaged and the average values are tested.

3.5 Object Detection & Tracking

(a) With Shadows (b) Normal

Figure 3.50: Lateral Object Detection and Tracking Results

Fig. 3.50(b) shows the results of lateral object detection. The two lateral search regions are marked as green rectangles at the left and at the right of the picture. Their absolute vertical limits (computed from the results of the lane detection) are marked as small white horizontal lines above the two regions. Due to the 8x8 averaging, the position and height of the detection areas for lateral object detection are rounded to multiples of 8. The detection regions are dynamically updated in each cycle (their vertical position is set using the results from the lane detection; their size is automatically adjusted to exclude the lane markings if necessary).

The detected candidate is shown in green using two lines that mark its vertical and horizontal limits. The vertical limit is determined as the transition from the road to a darker region, the horizontal area is the opposite transition but in this case the search direction is horizontal to the middle of the image. In both cases the coordinates are rounded to a multiple of 8. The finer positioning is done through the lateral object tracking algorithm.

In fig. 3.50(a) is shown an extreme case in which the shadows greatly influence the scene. Still, there is no problem in case of such big shadows since the strongest transition remains the one from the tyres to the shadowed area. The other challenge emerges when smaller shadows are caused by the sun high in the sky (noon time shadows). But, in this case, the shadows are also reduced in intensity. Even if their size would be wrongly detected, during the transition to the normal tracking model the size will be checked again and, if necessary, corrected.

The lateral candidates are passed directly to the specific lateral tracking algorithms with no additional filtering step.

Chapter 3

3.5.6 Object Detection - Distant/Far Objects

The detection of far candidates is accomplished using a simple edge detector. The algorithm is simplistic; it searches for horizontal edges of an arbitrary width (6-12 pixels was used). The exact width is not relevant by itself; it may be arbitrary chosen. It is important that the width in the middle of the range ($\frac{6+12}{2} = 9$) is the same as the width of the far objects that are allowed to change the position of the search rows.

After a successful detection the result is validated before being transmitted further by checking the form of the candidate (against a template image; by using the same template matching algorithm as for the tracking). This ensures that big horizontal structures (shadows, road patches, large traffic shields, etc.) are dropped from the result set.

(a) Search Rows

(b) Results

Figure 3.51: Far Object Detection

The search region for the detection of the far candidates would be ideally a single row (the row in which the far objects have the average width equal to the middle of the allowed width range). Its position is dynamically defined using information from already tracked objects. Due to pitch angle variations and the vertical curvature of some streets, the search region cannot be restricted to a single row. Few close rows are searched; this ensures that even in case of pitch angle variations or non flat roads the far vehicles remain in one of the searched rows, therefore generating candidates. To speed up the algorithm and to avoid generating too many candidates for a single object, the distance between two rows is about 4 pixels. The layout of the search rows is illustrated in fig. 3.51(a).

In fig. 3.51(b) is presented a typical false positive. Due to the perspective effect, the side delimiter of the road has a horizontal area of the expected width. This could be filtered out by the detection algorithm, provided that there are no vertical edges at its ends. Unfortunately, this is not the case. Both ends have vertical edges; both of them belonging to the infrastructure. This is a case that cannot be eliminated by the single frame analysis of the detection algorithms for distant objects. It will be eliminated during the tracking because its form will change (it is composed of objects situated at different depths that will respect the motion parallax law).

Before delivery, a candidate object is classified as passenger car or truck by means of the relative height of its vertical edges with respect to its width. Most trucks are built with the maximum allowed dimensions for such vehicles, i.e. their width is 2,55 m and their height is 4 m (or very close to those dimensions). The presence of a horizontal edge that links the two vertical edges (the top of the truck is much better defined as than that of small cars) counts as an extra valuable information.

The far candidates are passed directly to the specific far tracking algorithms with no additional filtering step.

3.5.7 Filtering the Candidates

The obtained candidates from the SI metrics or road detection results are filtered to reduce the large number of false positives as illustrated in Fig. 3.45. The filters are additive (logic and). In other words, it is enough that an object is filtered by one filter to be deleted from the result set passed to the tracking algorithms.

The first filter uses a width based criterion. The width of an object should not be larger on that image row than the recognized lane width or smaller than one fourth of it (the filter is implemented using pixel measurements, no 3D information is necessary). For the general reference, in 3D this would mean that the car width should be somewhere between 90 cm to 360 cm. This range is so generous, that the real objects will not be affected, but large shadows areas or tiny false positives will be eliminated from the result set. This filter is active only if the lane recognition is active.

The second filter removes false positives generated by vegetation. The color segmentation method based on the SI metric labels any pixel that is not similar to road or markings as a possible "candidate point". The vegetation is usually dense and thus has a higher percentage (the threshold used is 90%) of its area covered with candidate points. This property allows the removal of false positives generated at both sides of the road. A typical car has always black (e.g. tyres, lower chassis elements) or white/silver regions (e.g. handles, rear lights, license plate, chrome inserts), as well as glass areas that generate less coverage as a pure vegetation area.

For highway scenarios a third filter was implemented. It is based on the fact that the backlights of the cars are red, therefore a minimum of few red points with at least average saturation should be present on the footprint of the objects in the image. Since the filter "successfully" removes all objects belonging to the incoming traffic on the country roads, and newly it has also problems with the backlights using LED technology - which are not only white but also a beloved design trend at the moment of this thesis - it was disabled in this form and implemented as an additional hint in the tracking algorithms.

Some examples of filtered objects were shown in fig. 3.48(b) and in fig. 3.49(b). As it can be seen, the filters are not very strict, but still efficiently remove about 30% - 70% of the false positives. The rest of the false positives will be removed by the tracking algorithms themselves.

Chapter 3

3.5.8 Tracking of Objects - Lateral Objects

The lateral object tracking algorithm is almost trivial due to the fact that the detection of lateral candidates is very stable. Only two issues are to be solved by the tracking algorithm: removing false positives generated by shadows and compensating for misses due to small detection areas or particularities of the object that do not match the features used for the detection.

The shadow problem is solved by analyzing the extent of the edge present under the object. Objects have the property of entering the picture slowly coming from lateral positions. Shadows come suddenly in the picture and have a greater extent. The footprint movement is nothing else but the relative speed difference (a shadow has the opposite ego velocity, while an object is typically much slower).

Practically if an object suddenly enters the picture (it was not yet tracked), it will only be considered if its width is smaller than 18 pixels (5% of the image width). If not, no tracked object will be created. When a saved image sequence is started from a position with a lateral object that is already half present in the picture, it will be ignored. This problem cannot appear in live tests, except when the system is to be started (or reseted) in the middle of the driving test. But in this case all system parameters (lane detection, average SI values for lane and road, lateral regions etc.) have probably not yet converged to stable values, therefore missing a lateral object is not at all relevant.

The missed detections are compensated for by running the detection algorithm in the already known lower area of the object. When this test fails, the object is dropped. Therefore the lateral tracking algorithm does a simple re-detection. This makes the algorithm extremely dynamic. Since the scope of the system presented in this thesis is limited only to the assertion of the existence of the lateral objects, tracking them in 3D coordinates makes no sense (their 3D coordinates remain constant).

3.5.9 Tracking of Objects - New Objects

Once an object was detected by one of the algorithms in 3.5.3 or in 3.5.4 and made it to the filtering algorithms described in 3.5.7, it is passed to those algorithms that have to accomplish two major tasks:

- position properly the object using the image information;
- assert the existence probability for the object and if necessary trigger the model change so that the object can be outputted as soon as possible.

As it can be seen the tasks are not at all different from the tasks of any typical tracking algorithm. The reason for which these tracking algorithms were not simply implemented in the regular tracking algorithm, is that the object detection is not very exact, therefore the limits for the position adjustment are much larger for new objects. The second reason is that integrating both models would generate a "monster" model that would be considerably hard to debug.

The object positioning is based on the already known SI segmentation algorithm. The metric is the one from 3.10. The row situated 6 pixels under the object (empirically

3.5 Object Detection & Tracking

determined from measurements so that the shadows and tyres of the detected vehicle remain typically above this line) is taken as the reference for the "bad" values. I.e. the S,I values of the pixel for which the SI metric value is the minimum of all pixels on the line is chosen as the bad point. The "good" SI values are learned from previously successfully tracked new objects. They start with S = 128 and I = 0. The divider and the threshold are dynamically evaluated using the algorithm described in 3.11.

(a) Width and Align Algorithm

(b) New Objects

Figure 3.52: SI Metric for Object Alignment of the Newly Detected Objects

Fig. 3.52(a) presents the results of running the metric and thresholding the points on 12 rows (but not more than the $\frac{objectheight}{4}$) above the given object bottom. A histogram is build with the number of points on a column that have the metric values above the threshold. The biggest outer peaks on the histogram are probably corresponding to the left and right tyre. They are chosen as the left and right delimiters. The lowest row at these columns for which the metric returns a value at least equal to the threshold is used for the bottom of the object. The height of the object is set by default to be equal to 80% of the object width (this value was computed from the height of the passenger cars in the compact class). The fig. 3.52(b) shows the results of the positioning. Two of the objects were already passed to the regular tracking model.

The width positioning algorithm does fails when (i) the new computed object width is smaller than 3 pixels or (ii) the two maximum values in the histogram are smaller than the $\frac{1}{4}$ of the theoretical maximum (i.e. the height of the region to which the SI metric is applied). If the width positioning algorithm fails, then a simpler algorithm is tried. It only positions the bottom of the object (but no horizontal alignment is done). The bottom of the object is set as the lowest row in a region with a height of 16 pixels, centred on the detected lower part of the object containing no metric result bigger than the threshold.

If the width positioning algorithm is successful, the object is passed to the regular (or lateral) tracking model. The difference between this tracking model and the detection method based on the SI metric is that, while the detection method does suppose that the object is different from the road and accordingly uses the road average values, this algorithm supposes that the object is detected and uses the tyre values and the area below the detected object. The two algorithms are similar, but the tracking algorithm is more limited with respect to the impact that it may have on position and size of the detected object.

(a) New Object Tracking Model

(b) Specific Tracking Model

Figure 3.53: Transition to Specific Tracking Model

It is also important to understand the way the detected object data is fed into the tracking algorithms. In fig. 3.45 is presented the rare situation when an object cannot be associated to any already tracked object, therefore will generate a new object with the model for new objects. In reality this will not happen for objects multiply detected. The association step is run before all tracking algorithms are run. In the association step each tracking model gets each detected object and has to answer the question "can this detected object be associated to one of the objects tracked with this tracking model?". If the question is answered affirmatively than the candidate is removed from the list of detected objects and the corresponding tracked object can use the information carried by the detected object to update its position and/or trust. Additionally at the end of each cycle all of the tracked objects are checked to remove duplicates (one single physical object being tracked with more models).

In fig. 3.53(a) and fig. 3.53(b) are presented the results of running the tracking algorithms multiple times on the same frame. The objects belonging to the "new object" model are marked in light violet, to the regular model in yellow, to the far model in green.

In the first run six new objects are detected. One is promoted in the same cycle to the regular tracking model, the other five still remain in the "new object" tracking model. The algorithms run 10 times on the same image. The detected objects (candidate list) remain almost the same. Due to available lane information the right most candidates will be filtered over its size and disappears from the result set. The other two distant objects switch to regular tracking model and in the same cycle are passed to the distant/far tracking model. The corresponding candidates are being associated in the association step and disappear from the result set. The other two (left most new objects in 3.53(a)) will be associated to the left most car and will be deleted from the new object model. The corresponding candidates are also associated during each cycle and will not generate any objects in the "new object" tracking model. Summing up, no object will remain in the "new object" model since all the candidates can be properly associated to already existing objects in other models.

The objects belonging to the "new object" model are never outputted on the CAN. They can only be displayed in the CCVS debug application.

3.5.10 Tracking of Regular Objects - up to about 70 meters

The algorithms of the regular object tracking model use mostly intensity information and the positioning is done in smaller intervals as in the case of the "new object" tracking model. Technically, a fine horizontal positioning is performed, followed by a complex and precise vertical positioning.

The horizontal positioning is based on the fact that a car that is on the road generates two symmetric transitions (at left, respectively at right) from lighter values (due to road) to darker values (due to tyre), respectively vice versa. These two transitions are close as value and if the search area is small enough they are the maximum transitions in the region due to the fact that cars usually have a relatively uniform horizontal intensity.

(a) Horizontal (b) Vertical

Figure 3.54: Tracking the positioning for regular objects

The algorithm works by computing the vertical sums in an image band situated around the current vertical position and choosing one out of the two most significant transitions in the average intensity for each lateral side of the car. The decision is validated by taking into account the previous width and position of the car and of its backlights (if detected).

Chapter 3

This approach avoids interpreting false transitions due to other objects or lane markings as lateral limits for the current object.

The horizontal positioning algorithm steps are: (i) choose a region that should be small enough to avoid noises and big enough to contain a possibly displaced object; (ii) compute intensity sum on each vertical strip (iii) find maximum transition left/right from light-to-dark/dark-to-light. If one of the maximum transitions do not confirm the object width (the width is considered constant and the other detected margin is used to get the reference point) but the second maximum confirms it, than choose the second maximum position. This is illustrated in fig. 3.54(a). This helps in stabilizing the results when the car drives close to the markings. If the transitions are similar and the change in size is reasonable, then the new left/right peaks give the positions of the transitions.

The vertical positioning is based on the fact that a car on the road generates two symmetric transitions (left, respectively right) from lighter road values to darker tyres values when processing the picture from bottom to top. These two transitions have close values and if the search area is small enough, they are the maximum transitions in the region.

Two issues are related to this algorithm: (i) it does not work in heavy rain conditions due to the sprayed water at the contact of the tyres with the ground (ii) it has to be corrected for shadows, otherwise the position will always get stuck with shadows that generate stronger contrast with the illuminated road as the tyres with the shadow.

The vertical positioning also takes into account the results of the road detection, the change in the position of the backlights (if detected) and the image itself. It handles cases of a car entering/exiting from a strong horizontal shadow, cases of poor visibility of the contact surface of the tyres (or partial occlusions), cases of false positives due to lane markings (as in fig. 3.54(b)) and cases of strong breaking in which the car suddenly approaches the bottom of the picture.

(a) Source Image   (b) Road Detection and Objects

Figure 3.55: Handling shadows during the tracking of regular objects

3.5 Object Detection & Tracking

The steps of the vertical positioning algorithm are: (i) choose a region that should be small enough to avoid noises and big enough to contain a possibly displaced object; (ii) find maximum intensity transitions on the vertical positions for left and right. If the two transitions are not close enough, but one of them is close (empirically set to cover a relative speed of about 25 m/s) to the previous car position, then ignore the distant one and use the close one as result. If the two transitions are very similar in value then return their average vertical position (rounded up) as the result.

The shadows are handled with two separate algorithms.

The first method interprets the road detection results. The road detection itself (as presented in 3.4.2) handles the problem of shadows. If the area in the shadow under the car was detected as road (due to the shadow handling routines), then the vertical position is the one given by the road detection (in fig. 3.55(b) it can be seen how the road detection handles the shadows).

(a) Source Image   (b) Object Tracking

Figure 3.56: Tracking backlights to assist regular object tracking

The second method is based on the detection of backlights. The problem with the shadow does only apply to cars having a positive relative velocity (otherwise they will cover the shadow in the next frame). Therefore detecting backlights is a perfectly suited solution in this particular case as illustrated in fig. 3.56(a). The detection of backlights gives, beside other relevant information, the vertical position of the backlights. The position is tracked between the frames. If the backlights indicate that the new position is closer to the top of the image as the position obtained by the vertical position algorithm, the results of the vertical position are dropped. Fig. 3.56(b) depicts this situation. The car is entering the shadow and even if the vertical positioning will tend to stick with the shadow margin (because it is stronger and closer to the position of the car in the previous frame), the backlight tracking accurately tracks the car. In this particular situation the road detection is working very well and confirms the results of the backlight tracking algorithm.

Chapter 3

A second application of the detection of the backlights is to handle the high dynamic cases such as strong braking. Typically, the limits of the movement of a vehicle inside a frame are set to cover a relative speed of about 10 m/s (36 km/h). These limits are ignored if all three methods (vertical position, backlight tracking and road detection) return the same results.

The final step in the tracking normal objects is to find out the 3D width of the vehicle using the ratio of its width to the width of the lane at that position (from the lane tracking output). These results are filtered over time to provide the distant object tracking with an accurate estimate of the 3D object width. This information is later used in computing the distance to objects that are too far to be reconstructed with triangulation methods.

3.5.11 Tracking of Distant/Far Objects - beyond about 70 meters

Particularities of Far Objects

By a far car or object it is understood a car that is no wider than 24 pixels. For the camera setup used in this article (a horizontal focal length of 996 pixels) this corresponds to about 70 meters for a vehicle (passenger car) that has a width of 170 cm, respectively 105 meters for a vehicle (truck) that has a width of 255 cm.

One issue encountered in far object detection and tracking is that values for saturation and color corresponding to cars that are between 10 and 24 pixels wide are very noisy. Even if more accurate, the intensity information is not always reliable. Besides, the accuracy of the lateral position of a detected car is limited by the image resolution. The high dynamic of the pitch angle characteristic to any system mounted in a car poses an additional challenge. This materializes in sudden vertical movements of the objects in the image. Even in cases of lane change manoeuvres, due to the frame rate of 25 fps, the horizontal movement of a car into the picture remains relatively small.

One positive aspect is that all far cars, being very small in the picture, generate a very similar footprint. This makes the use of template matching algorithms possible. Another positive aspect is related to the horizontal edge generated in the picture under a car. The edge is better defined as in the case when the footprint of the car is wider (the edge consistency can be modified in the latter case by the cast shadow under the car or the road texture).

Multi-Method Approach for Tracking Far Objects

The input for the tracking methods consists of the position, width and type (car/truck) of the object.

More methods are used to track an already detected candidate in a sequence of images. The search intervals for all these methods are fixed. They are empirically estimated using data from several test sequences. The following methods are independent of the prior detection, i.e. once detected, a candidate can be tracked without additional hints from the detection. Four algorithms are used, one of them (positioning based on edge detection) only as a temporary "rescue" solution when the other three (image correlation,

3.5 Object Detection & Tracking

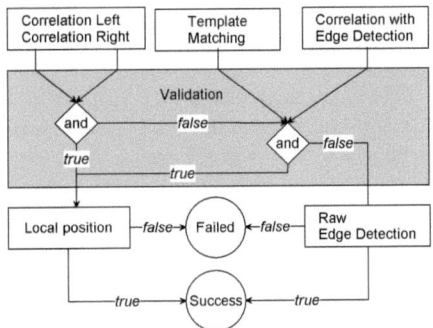

Figure 3.57: Software Diagram for Far Object Tracking

template matching and edge image correlation) do not deliver consistent results. Fig. 3.57 shows the connections between the four algorithms. If the tracking succeeds using the three main methods, a post validation and exact positioning is performed. In order not to influence the results of the detection, the regions of interest used are tiny (2 pixels on each side of the detected position). The four methods are presented in detail in the next paragraphs.

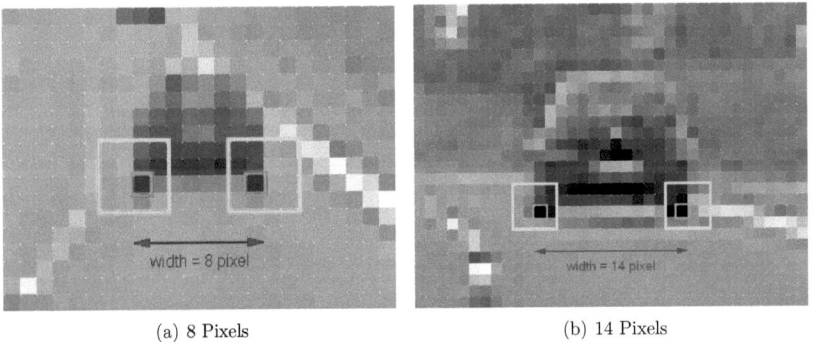

(a) 8 Pixels (b) 14 Pixels

Figure 3.58: Correlation Areas

Correlation: For the sake of speed, there is no copy of the whole previous frame for the correlation. Each object saves its region of interest for the future processing. All possible object points were tested for the stability of the correlation over time. The points situated on the lateral sides of the object performed the best, in particular at the bottom of the tyres. The result is not surprising since a relatively small (4x4 pixels) correlation

109

Chapter 3

region is used (see Fig. 3.58). For this size of the region, the differences between street and tyres compensate the small signal/noise ratio.

The correlation is carried out at the bottom of the left and of the right tyre, at the exterior of the car (see Fig. 3.58). The limits of the search area were experimentally estimated by finding the biggest movement of several targets into typical sequences. The correlation function is the absolute difference $(abs(Intensity_{leftimage}(x,y) - Intensity_{rightimage}(x,y))$. There was little benefit from using more complex correlation functions (due to the small correlation area).

If the width of the object suffers no significant change and both correlation values are good, than the correlation is successful and the result goes to the fine positioning algorithm. By correlation value is to be understood the similarity between averaged intensity differences for the left and right areas.

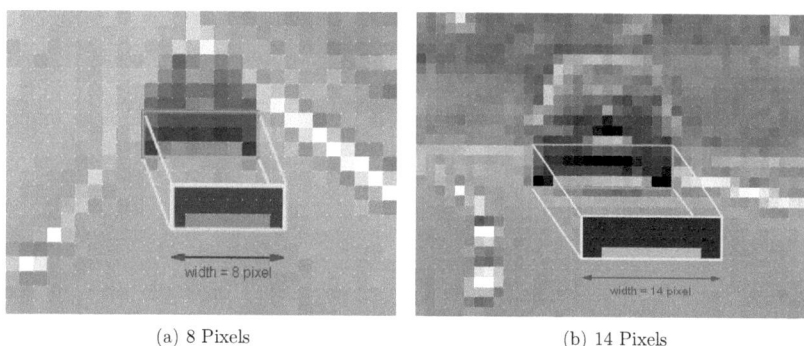

(a) 8 Pixels   (b) 14 Pixels

Figure 3.59: Detection Templates and Corresponding Samples

Template matching: The template matching (Fig. 3.59) is performed with a dynamically generated template as long as the width of the object is bigger as 13 pixels. The smaller templates were manually created, analyzing sequences of images, to fine tune their form. Each template is stored as a mask. It will be filled in with actual values obtained from the street detection algorithms and later from the object itself (values obtained in the previous frame). This ensures an auto adaptation of the template to local properties of the region in which the object lies and improves the robustness of the method.

Edge Based Correlation: Due to the relative high number of edges belonging to the object in the search region, one may expect a better result for the correlation if performed on the image obtained by convoluting with an edge operator. Unfortunately, due to the small signal/noise ratio, the correlation on the gradient image is no better than the correlation on the original image. More complicated edge extraction algorithms were also tested, but the average performance remained below the one of the correlation on the source image. Still, the edge based correlation cannot be ignored in cases in which significant image changes occur (e.g. the tracked object enters a shadow). Therefore it is

3.5 Object Detection & Tracking

(a) Beginning (b) End

Figure 3.60: Object tracking example

used to stabilize the results from the correlation and template matching.

Raw Edge Positioning: If all three methods fail or generate different results, in order to keep the object alive for few frames, a horizontal and after that a vertical align algorithm similar to the one for regular objects is used. The only difference is that the search regions are smaller.

Besides the used methods, an important aspect is the validation of the correlation or template matching results. All of the three described methods may generate false results in cases when foreign structures or shadows are present in their search area. For example, when an object crosses a lane marking, the position on the marking has no match in the previous picture. Such cases are eliminated in a post validation step.

Fig. 3.57 shows the algorithm flow. Roughly, the results of the best performing method (image correlation) are evaluated (with respect to the individual correlation results on left and right). If the results match the output is generated. If not they are checked against the results of the template matching and edge image correlation. If a good match between the results of two out of three methods could be found, the output is generated. In case that the results of all three methods look different, the "rescue" positioning solution is used to eventually carry the object for one or two extra frames. If the correlation for the next frames fails, the object will be dropped.

Fig. 3.60 shows an example in which the algorithm tracked a Volkswagen Phaeton car for more than 900 frames. After that, the Phaeton will get closer, switch to regular model, to lateral model and finally leave the field of view.

The test sequences showed that tracking a car in a highway scenario is successful in good weather conditions until the car is about 8 pixels wide (with frequent cases in which a car was tracked until it was 6 pixels wide). In bad weather conditions the algorithm may become unstable under 12 pixels. For the current camera setup (focal length of 996 pixels on X axis) a width of 8 pixels for a real width of 170 cm (typical passenger car

Chapter 3

width) corresponds to about 210 meters, while one of 12 pixels corresponds to about 140 meters.

4 Reconstructing 3D information

4.1 Motivation

In almost all driver assistance applications the output of the vision sensor is implicitly required in 3D coordinates for at least two reasons: (i) data correlation with other sensors (radar, laserscanner) and (ii) requirements from the controller of car dynamics.

This chapter deals with the reconstruction of 3D lane and object information from the detection results in the picture.

4.2 Requirements for the Output of a Vision Sensor for Automotive Applications

The traffic lane is commonly modeled as a clothoid in the 3D space along with a width and position relative to the car coordinate system [81].

$$X = c_1 * \frac{Z^3}{6} + c_0 * \frac{Z^2}{2} + \tan(-\alpha) * Z + X_0 \qquad (4.1)$$

In (4.1) the coefficients mean: X_0 - position of the ego car in the lane; α - heading angle; Z - the depth at which the horizontal position is computed; c_0 - curvature; c_1 - curvature variation. The equation of the clothoid is presented in (4.1). If the vertical profile is required then to this horizontal description a second clothoid is added to describe the behaviour of the road in the vertical plane.

Not all coefficients are always used by driver assistance systems. Typically only some of the following parameters are estimated:
- width of the lane
- horizontal curvature and curvature variation
- lateral displacement of the car with respect to the center of the lane (or vice versa)
- angles (yaw -yaw and yaw-rate can also be obtained from car electronics like ESP-, maybe pitch)

Lane departure warning systems use either the "time to line crossing" (TLC) or the comparison between current angles between the car projection and interpolations of detected lane markings. Both of these values can be computed directly out of the image coordinates [102], respectively [52], therefore are not analyzed in this paper.

In case of a lane keeping system the most relevant input is the lateral displacement. The heading angle and/or the curvature can be used to stabilize the controller loop or to improve the controller reaction.

Chapter 4

The width, lateral displacement and curvature (sometimes also the curvature variation) are used to associate objects detected with other sensors to a certain traffic lane.

Objects are represented as cuboids in the 3D space, characterized by their geometry, position and dynamics. Their position is characterized by a point in the chosen 3D coordinate system (Lateral: X, Vertical: Y, Depth: Z), their geometry usually simplified to cuboids dimensions (Width: W, Height: H, Length: L) and their dynamics reduced to relative speed (S) or acceleration (A) information.

Out of this information the most important are Z, X and S. X and Z allow the object/lane association. S allows the prediction of the object movement. Since S and A cannot be measured directly by a vision sensor (like S in case of radar), they are derived over time and therefore they do not belong to the subject of this paper.

Summing up, this chapter focuses on how to reconstruct the curvature, width of lane, lateral position of the ego, X and Z object coordinates. These are the most used parameters in automotive applications.

4.3 Projections of the 3D space in the image plane

The pinhole camera model used is presented in detail in [102]. Assuming no radial distortions, the 3D clothoid equation and the position of a point in the 3D space are projected through the intrinsic camera calibration matrix into the image plane. This implies that the world coordinate system is the camera coordinate system. Otherwise, making the general projection would bring such level of complexity that would make the equation impossible to solve for practical purposes. Transforming the equation later to the desired coordinate system makes the whole task not only simpler, but allows for the free choice of the common coordinate system for all sensors.

In the following equations the symbols used mean: F_x and F_y - focal length expressed as a measure of the width, respectively height of the pixel; O_x and O_y - horizontal and vertical coordinate of the projection of the principal point onto the image plane; X_i and Y_i coordinates into the image plane (relative to bottom/left position into the picture); X_c, Y_c and Z_c coordinates of a point in the camera coordinate system.

$$X_i = O_x - F_x * \frac{X_c}{Z_c}, \qquad Y_i = O_y - F_y * \frac{Y_c}{Z_c} \qquad (4.2)$$

Projection of a single point. Projecting a 3D point from the camera coordinate system (X_c, Y_c, Z_c) into image coordinates [102] (X_i, Y_i) leads to the equations presented in (4.2). Remarks:

- measuring a width $(X_{c1} - X_{c2})$ at the same Z_c will reduce the principal point projection from the equation as shown in (4.3)

$$X_{i1} - X_{i2} = F_x * \frac{X_{c1} - X_{c2}}{Z_c} \qquad (4.3)$$

- one may associate to a row of the image a pixel/meter coefficient that is constant in world coordinate system, as well, if all points having the same Z_c and Y_c project on the

same image row (i.e. changes in camera height, pitch and roll angle remain small)
- projection formulas give no direct way to compute Z_c (since Z_c is the normalizing factor)

$$\begin{bmatrix} -F_x & 0 & O_x \\ 0 & -F_y & O_y \\ 0 & 0 & 1 \end{bmatrix} \begin{bmatrix} a*Z_c^3 + b*Z_c^2 + c*Z_c + d \\ Y_c \\ Z_c \end{bmatrix} \quad (4.4)$$

Projection of a clothoid. In the flat road assumption, projecting the clothoid onto the image plane is the same as computing the product in (4.4) and normalizing with the element in the third row(Z_c).

$$\begin{bmatrix} -a*F_x*Z_c^2 - b*F_x*Z_c - \frac{d*F_x}{Z_c} + O_x - c*F_x \\ O_y - \frac{Y_c*F_y}{Z_c} \\ 1 \end{bmatrix} \quad (4.5)$$

The result is presented in (4.5). This vector is in fact $[X, Y, 1]_T$. In order to obtain an equation in image coordinates, the variable Z_c is expressed as a function of Y_i and replaced in the expression for X_i. $Y_i - O_y$ is factored out and denoted for the sake of simplicity with Y_{ri}. Similarly X_{ri} denotes $X_i - O_x$.

$$-\frac{Y_c^2 * a * F_y^2}{Y_{ri}^2} + \frac{Y_c * b * F_y}{Y_{ri}} + \frac{d * Y_{ri}}{Y_c * F_y} - c = \frac{X_{ri}}{F_x} \quad (4.6)$$

Equation (4.6) presents the final expression in which the only extrinsic variable is the height of the 3D marking points (Y_c).

One may suggest that if the curvature is not required then position and lane width information can be obtained using a simplified description in which only the last 2 terms are involved. It is more convenient to use a simpler method that can be calibrated directly to world coordinates. It computes the distance to the lane marking as the lateral distance to a point of the 3D space (like for the lateral displacement of the objects).

That is, using (4.3) and the assumption that a specific row of the image corresponds to a road section having Z_c and Y_c constant, all that is needed additionally is to have a reference point and a pixel per meter coefficient associated to this row. The reference point is taken to be the position of the point having $X_c = 0$.

4.4 Reconstruction of 3D Information

Ego Lateral Position. As presented in fig. 4.1 the method is directly derived from (4.3). Assuming that all points of the street having the same Y_c and Z_c will project on the same image row (i.e. flat road and negligible dynamic changes in pitch angle and camera height above the ground), one arbitrary image row is chosen (in the lower part of the image to benefit from the improved resolution). The image point on this row that has $X_c = 0$ (denoted by X_{ic0}) and the factor pixels/meter (denoted with C_{ppm}) are the

Chapter 4

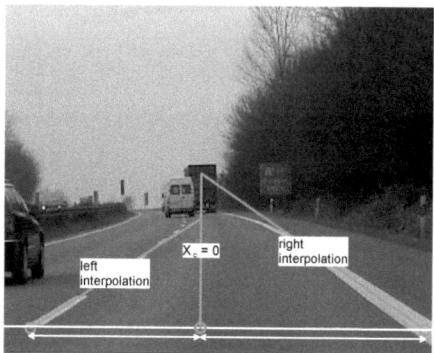

Figure 4.1: Estimating the ego lateral position

only two required parameters. If the positive X axis points to the left then one may write for a certain X_i position on that particular image row (4.7):

$$X_c = \frac{X_{ic0} - X_i}{C_{ppm}} \qquad (4.7)$$

The prerequisites (flat road, negligible dynamic changes in pitch angle and camera height) proved to be reasonable for automotive applications. Due to the oscillatory characteristic of the vertical movement of the car, the dynamic changes can also be filtered out well over time.

If the coordinates are expressed in the world coordinate system the only required modification is that the two parameters (C_{ppm} and X_{xc0}) must be calibrated/computed in this coordinate system as well.

Lane Width. Using the same parameters as in the case of the lateral position of the ego vehicle, the computation of the lane width is straight forward. The absolute difference of the two positions of the left and right lane delimiters gives the lane width.

One may also reconstruct the width starting from (4.2). In this case a depth must be assigned to an arbitrary image row during the calibration process and F_x must be known. The method is just another form of the prior one.

Object Lateral Position. Two solutions for obtaining the lateral position of an object are discussed. The first uses the same approach as in the case of the in-lane position.

The advantage is that the lateral distance does not depend explicitly on the distance.

The disadvantages are:

- the C_{ppm} and X_{xc0} factors have to be computed for each image row in which objects are present
- the dynamic movements of the car may introduce significant reconstruction errors with the distance.

4.4 Reconstruction of 3D Information

Both disadvantages can be compensated if the interpolation of the lane in the image generates the C_{ppm} coefficient using the information that at a specific row in the image the width of the current lane is known in both meters (filtered over time) and pixels. I.e. a virtual lane with no curvature and heading straight ahead is taken and the relative position of the object point with respect to the lane together with the lane information is giving the position information.

The second solution is to use the depth information for an object and to compute X_c from the equation (4.2).

The advantage is that only the O_x and F_x parameters are required.

The disadvantage is the dependency induced between Z_c and X_c. All errors of reconstruction of the Z_c parameter will be found in X_c as well.

Depth. Two methods of reconstructing depth information for objects are discussed.

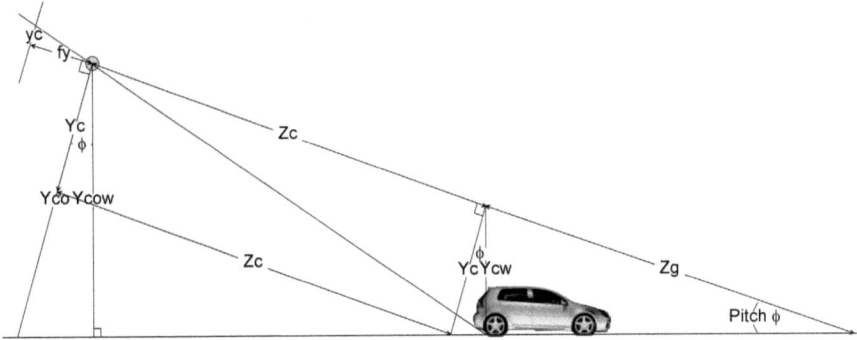

Figure 4.2: Depth estimation using object baseline

In fig. 4.2 is presented the common approach (similar to [51]) that uses for the computation the distance in picture from the base of image to the base of the object. The pitch angle is exaggerated in order to make the figure readable. The formula is (under the assumption that the road in front of the camera is flat; everything being expressed in camera coordinates):

$$Z_c = \frac{Y_{C0} * F_y}{y_c + F_y * tan(\phi)} \quad (4.8)$$

In (4.8) the not yet described symbols mean: Y_{C0} height of the camera above ground in camera reference system; ϕ is the pitch angle; y_c is the distance in image on the Y axis between the principal point and the base of the object.

Unfortunately this approach is sensitive to pitch angle movements and has a very poor resolution near the focal point of the camera ($tan(\alpha)$ is closed to 0 for small pitch angles and y_c is an integer value with limited resolution around 0). This makes it unsuitable for example in far object scenarios. In this case the pitch angle movements generate

Chapter 4

significant computation errors due to the variation they induce in the object position on y. Unfortunately in a typical forward looking camera setup the object base for far objects lies near the optical center position.

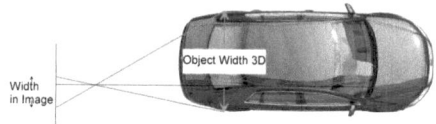

Figure 4.3: Depth estimation using object width

In fig. 4.3 is presented a different approach. It is simple and robust, but it has one major drawback. The width of the object (in meters) is required. This problem can be addressed in several ways:

- supposing that the current lane has a constant width, one can use the $\frac{objectwidth}{lanewidth}$ report and the current lane size to find out the width

- use the width that was obtained with other methods as long as the object was in a different range (e.g. (4.8))

- assume a constant width (at a higher level use more width classes and choose between them based on image analysis)

In case of road vehicles (cars, trucks) the last assumption works the best. The width of a passenger car is supposed to be 170 cm (with a 10% error margin this covers practically all passenger cars produced in large series), respectively for trucks 255 cm. Of course, this induces a systematic error if the assumption does not hold, but the results are not only more stable, they remain in a typical 20% error margin for objects that are wider than 10 pixels (the error for the width is about 2 pixels). Also there is no dependency on the pitch angle variation.

$$Z_c = \frac{W_{3D}}{w_{img}} * F_x \qquad (4.9)$$

The corresponding depth computation formula is presented in (4.9). The newly introduced symbols mean: W_{3D} 3D width of the object (meters); w_{img} width of the object in image coordinates (pixels).

Curvature. In (4.6) making the assumption that the road is flat and that the camera pitch angle is very small, the position of all road points used to estimate the curvature may be approximated as the opposite of the camera height above the road. Using this assumption and the projection equation in (4.6), the method to compute the curvature is straight forward. One has to interpolate a curve of the form $a_0 * \frac{1}{Y_{ri}^2} + a_1 * \frac{1}{Y_{ri}} + a_2 * Y_{ri} + a_3 = X_{ri}$ from a set of points in the image. The values for c_0, c_1, α and X_0 are computed from $a_0, ..a_3$ knowing the intrinsic parameters and the height of the camera above ground 4.10.

$$c_1 = 6 * -\frac{a_0}{Y_c^2 * F_y^2 * F_x}, \quad c_0 = 2 * \frac{a_1}{Y_c * F_y * F_x}$$
$$\alpha_0 = \arctan(\frac{a_3}{F_x})$$
$$X_0 = \frac{a_2 * F_y * Y_c}{F_x} \tag{4.10}$$

4.5 Alternative Calibration Methods

Using the "standard" camera calibration model (intrinsic/extrinsic) and deriving the coefficients in the above presented equations may prove too difficult in a production environment due to the need to accurately calibrate each single camera. Even if the calibration process is automated, it remains time-consuming and inconvenient in series production. One solution is to use a simpler model derived directly from the equations. Such a model should be able to be calibrated online in a very simple manner (single image calibration would be ideal).

In case of the curvature the whole set of intrinsic parameters and the height of the camera above the ground has to be known. Such an auto calibration process is complex and beyond the intent of this paper.

In (4.7) the only two parameters are X_{ic0} and C_{ppm}. The two parameters can be found using a single image with a marked lane and defined ego position and orientation.

In (4.8), if one denotes $u = Y_{C0} * F_y$ and $v = tan(\phi) * F_y$, the number of coefficients is reduced to 2, i.e. they can be found having two or more known distance measurements. This is much simpler than carrying out a complete camera calibration. It can easily be automated. Moreover, when calibrating for the product of more classic parameters, singular errors in the parameter computation are not multiplied since the product value is calibrated as a single item.

In (4.9), the only coefficient is F_x. That means that this coefficient can be computed from a single measurement with known distances. If W_{3D} is big enough, the measurement can be carried out at depths comparable with the maximum range. This improves the results and performs an implicit compensation of the distortions induced by the optics (which were ignored in the camera model used in this paper due to the level of complexity they generate).

Of course, all coefficients can be computed with improved precision as the solution of an over determined system of equations resulting from more measurements.

4.6 Experimental Results

The detection of the lane width in a known scenario using the calibration method proposed in 4.4 to evaluate the influence of the dynamic changes into extrinsic parameters was

Chapter 4

performed. The error remained in a 10% error margin with a maximum deviation in the case of strong braking of 32 cms for a width of 350 cm.

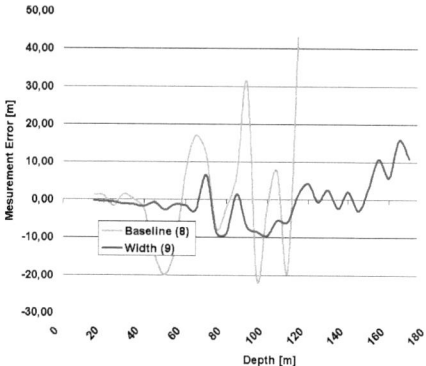

Figure 4.4: Errors in Depth reconstruction

In fig. 4.4 are presented the obtained distances for an object using the 2 proposed calibration methods. The measurements were performed on a flat road. The curve marked "Width" is interpolated from the results of the algorithm based on the car width. The "Baseline" curve is obtained by interpolating the results of the algorithm that uses the vertical position of the base of the object in the picture. The results in fig. 4.4 show clearly that the proposed depth computation method is very stable and outperforms the standard method for depths greater than 100 meters.

5 Results

5.1 System architecture

5.1.1 Software Environment

Development Tools and Software Platform

The targeted software platform is Microsoft Win32. Even if the image processing algorithms have no explicit dependency on WinAPI, the user interface was designed specifically for Win32.

All programs developed as part of this thesis were written using the BCB 6.0 IDE under Microsoft Windows XP®. BCB is a RAD IDE, that encapsulates most of the WinAPI complexities in a convenient, object oriented library, the VCL. Together with the relative simple user interface needed for the software system, this allowed for a focused development in which most of the time was spent implementing the specific image processing procedures.

Besides standard Windows user interface components, in order to comply with the real time requirements, the online application makes use of OpenGL to draw the results on the screen. Because virtually all OpenGL operations are performed by the GPU, they do not require processor time, allowing more time to be allocated for the processing task.

The IEEE 1394a based acquisition subsystem uses the exposed DirectX® 9 interfaces to get images from the camcorder.

System Architecture

The software system consists of the following applications:

Online Processing Application - CCVS-Online. It works online in the setup present in the car, processing images from an acquisition module (typically firewire camera) and outputting the results on the CAN bus. It uses an acquisition module from the ones described below. The graphical user interface is minimal. The application is multithreaded for maximum performance.

RGB2HSI Conversion Module (DLL). It converts the Red, Green, Blue (RGB) image representation to the Hue, Saturation, Intensity (HSI) format in realtime using a lookup table. Contains functions for the generation, saving and loading of the lookup table as well.

DV (firewire; 1394a) Capture Module (DLL). It captures images in real time from a standard IEEE 1394a/firewire camera (e.g. a consumer electronics camcorder) and

Chapter 5

makes them available for further processing. The underlying functionality is provided by Microsoft DirectX® 9.

Bitmap (offline; file based) Capture Module (DLL). It uses saved images to emulate an online acquisition module. It is used to perform tests on saved scenarios in order to ensure the reproducibility of test results.

Application Controller (Watchdog). It guarantees that the CCVS-Online stays running when software bugs generate unhandled exceptions. The controller communicates with CCVS-Online over TCP/IP and watches its activity. If running on the same machine it may also start, stop, restart or in extreme cases even kill CCVS-Online.

Offline Processing Application- CCVS-Dev. It is used for the development of the system. The exact same algorithms are used as for CCVS-Online, from the same set of source files. The application has a rich user interface, is single threaded to allow the best debugging conditions and runs only with saved bitmap sequences.

DV Capture. It acquires images from a standard IEEE 1394a camera and saves them to a specific directory on a hard drive as a bitmap sequence to use later with CCVS-Dev or the Offline Acquisition Module. The application allows the use of up to 4 separate temporary hard drives for output and of the whole available memory as buffers. Using such techniques it supports a maximum sustained frame rate of 25 fps for the standard PAL resolution of 720 x 576, 32 bit color with common PC hardware.

Documentation. The system has a complex and rich documentation from extended inline comments in doxygen format, detailed doxygen comments in extra .doxygen files up to PDF and other graphic rich formats. The documentation covers the complete system, special attention being paid to the algorithms. Standardized documentation like UML was preferred.

The most of the source code is contained in CCVS-Online and CCVS-Dev. Both share the same source files with respect to the algorithms, being different only in the GUI. The most important features of each of them are detailed in the next two subsections. A detailed description of their user interface can be found in the appendices, respectively their included user manuals in PDF format.

CCVS-Dev - Development Application

CCVS-Dev is used only for development purposes. Using the same source files for algorithms as CCVS-Online, it isolates its specific code by means of #ifdef blocks.

The application is single threaded in order to make the debug as simple as possible. It only works with saved sequences of bitmaps (for example with DV Capture), allowing step by step playback/reversed playback with detailed output. The results over imposed on images are actually written onto image data. These images can be saved and later used alone or in sequence for presentation purposes.

CCVS-Dev has an information-rich user interface as can be seen in Fig. 5.1. It is able to display from 3 up to 8 complete 360 x 288 images in conjunction with up to 2 large status memos on a screen resolution of 1280 x 1024. This allows checking each individual algorithm step with maximum efficiency in repeatable scenarios.

5.1 System architecture

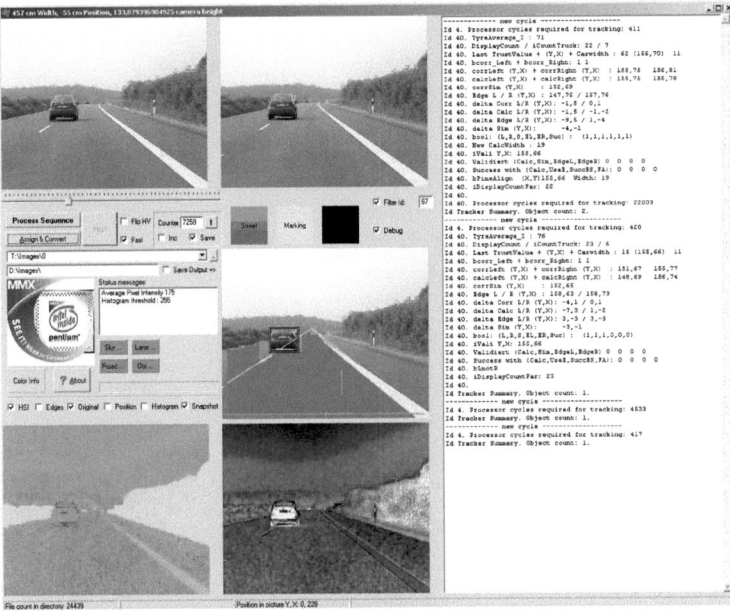

Figure 5.1: CCVS-Dev - GUI Interface

CCVS-Online - High-Performance Application

CCVS-Online was developed specially for the in-car usage. Even if it relies on the same processing code as the CCVS-Dev, its structure is not linear anymore. Additionally the intended image source is not relying anymore on bitmaps from the hard drive, but on an acquisition software module with a well defined interface. This module is using DirectX©9 interfaces to build and run an acquisition graph for generic firewire cameras or VCRs.

Due to the general approach for the acquisition, the CCVS-Online application can also run in off-line modus. Two options are available: (i) a VCR playing a tape recorded with the camera in the car or (ii) using bitmaps saved for CCVS-Dev with a specially developed file based acquisition module.

The application structure is presented in Fig. 5.2. The application starts by acquiring images together with associated CAN data, than carries out the processing that updates the internal environment representation, collects the output data, converts it to 3D information and finally outputs it on the CAN and on the output monitor (in the latter case over imposed on the source image).

Having a non-linear structure, the application is written in an event driven manner

123

Chapter 5

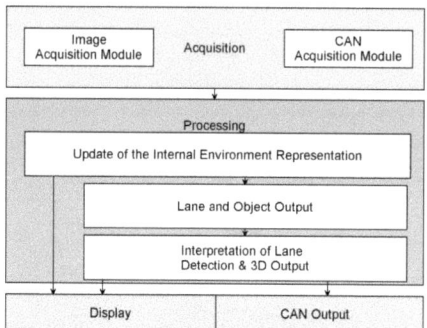

Figure 5.2: CCVS-Online - Basic Application Structure

in order to exploit optimally the system resources and to properly interfere with the image acquisition, display and the CAN bus drivers. It consists of multiple threads that are in charge of specialized tasks such as: responding to CAN events, acquiring images, outputting results and of course running the necessary image processing routines. The multitude of threads adds additional complexity to the application, but eliminates most dead-times due to synchronization with other devices and reallocates most of the interfacing to the dedicated devices as the graphics card, CAN card, etc. The exact calling order and thread tasks are detailed in the chapter dedicated to the processing algorithms.

5.1.2 Hardware Setup

In what follows the setup for the online application will be described in detail. The hardware required for CCVS-Dev is very simple, consisting of a single computer, therefore not subject to a detailed description.

System Diagram - CCVS-Online

The processing unit (car computer/laptop running CCVS) has a connection to a color mono camera over a firewire bus and to other systems (car controller, time generator, etc.) over CAN-Bus. The output of the system is sent over CAN-Bus or Ethernet to the driver assistance applications that require it.

The basic layout is described in Fig. 5.3. The camera and the firewire connection are described in the next section. The car controller delivers a lot of information about the ego vehicle from the built-in series sensors (like speed, yaw-rate, etc.). Out of this data, only the current ego speed (if present) is read and used. The time generator information consists of a unique timestamp used to synchronize all sensors present on the CAN Bus.

5.1 System architecture

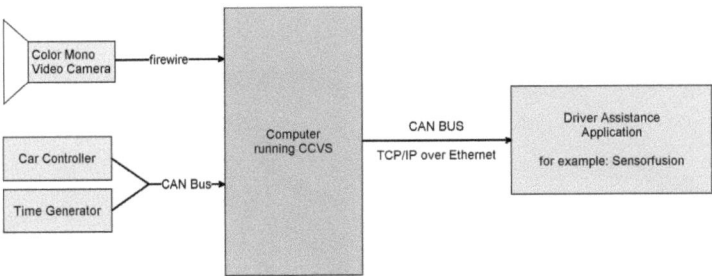

Figure 5.3: Basic Hardware Diagram

This timestamp is used to align the output of the CCVS results on the time axis of the sensor fusion system.

Color Vision Subsystem

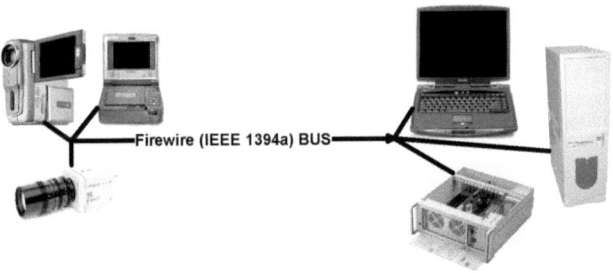

Figure 5.4: Image Acquisition and Processing - Hardware Options

The CCVS-Online uses a standard firewire interface to acquire images. This enables a very large spectrum (see Fig. 5.4) of both acquisition devices (industrial cameras, consumer electronics camcorders or even video walkmans) and target systems (specific car computers, laptops, standard desktop computers). The most common setup during the work for this thesis was a Sony PC109E camcorder together with a laptop or a dedicated car computer when available. The camcorder + laptop option was the most flexible one and, coupled with the very simple calibration required for the 3D reconstruction methods, allowed extremely quick and efficient installation of the system in any of the target vehicles.

125

Chapter 5

In-Car Setup

(a) The test vehicle

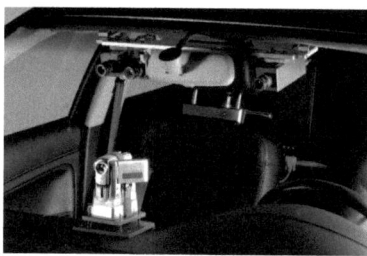
(b) Vision Sensors

Figure 5.5: In-Car Deployment Of Vision Sensors

The CCVS system was designed as a sensor for the INVENT project. The two test cars used were both Volkswagen Passat Variant. This subsection refers to the setup present in WOB VH-21 (see Fig. 5.5(a)). Fig. 5.5(b) shows the three vision sensors present in the car. The camera used by the CCVS system is the camcorder mounted below the other 3 cameras.

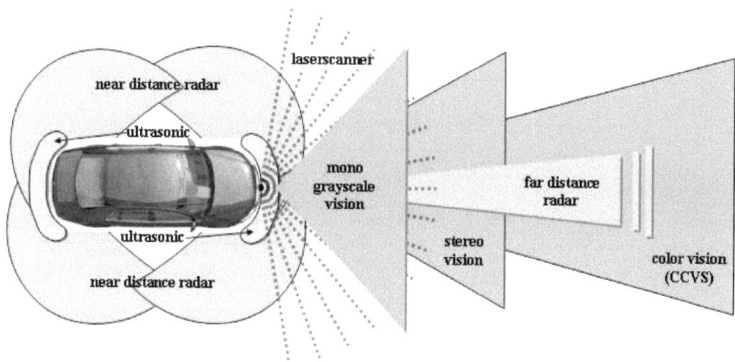

Figure 5.6: Sensors - deployment and range

In Fig. 5.6 is shown the installed sensors along with an approximate coverage of the space around the car. The sensors are:
- near radars (2 on the left side, 2 on the right side),
- laserscanner (ahead looking)
- far radar (ahead looking)
- greyscale stereo vision (the SCABOR system)

- greyscale mono vision (the AGLAIA system)
- color vision (CCVS).

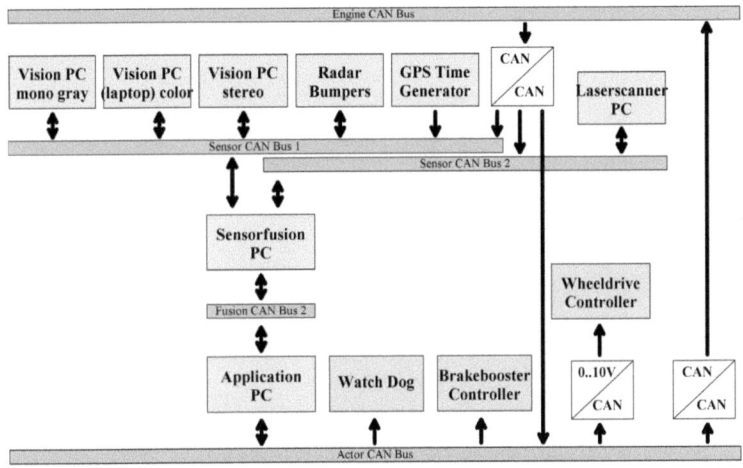

Figure 5.7: Interconnection Network over CAN

All these sensors were synchronized using a time generator and outputted their data on the CAN buses present in the car (see Fig. 5.7). Their output was fed into a sensor data fusion system which interpreted it and generated a higher level, detailed description of the environment. This description of the environment is used later to assist the driver and warn him/her of dangerous situations.

5.2 Results

This section is dedicated to the presentation of the most significant results achieved with the new methods introduced in this thesis. These results constitute the basis for the next chapter where the conclusions are drawn.

5.2.1 Hardware Platform

The system used for all the tests presented below is an IBM ThinkPad R52. Its hardware configuration is detailed below:
- Processor (CPU) Intel Pentium M Processor 750, 1.80GHz, 533MHz Front Side Bus
- Memory 512 MB
- Graphics chipset ATI Mobility RADEON x300, 64MB Video RAM
- Integrated Firewire Port (IEEE 1394)
- OS: Windows XP Professional, Service Pack 2

Chapter 5

5.2.2 Samples of the CCVS processing

This section presents results of the CCVS processing. The data is presented as outputted on the screen of the computer running the CCVS system and corresponds to the output written on CAN.

The focus remains on the object detection since this is the area in which the CCVS system has shown major improvements above other systems. The presentation here is not intended to be a complete or exhaustive one. It is meant to give a reader that unable to work directly with the system the possibility of evaluating at first glance the object detection in CCVS.

(a) Before the lane change   (b) After the lane change

Figure 5.8: Handling of a lane change situation

In fig. 5.8(a) and in fig. 5.8(b) is shown a typical lane change situation. At the bottom of the image, the lateral displacement is shown. The green bar at the bottom of fig. 5.8(a) shows that the ego vehicle is driving with a displacement to the right from the middle of the lane. The size of the bar is given by the number of centimetres in the displacement. It is directly converted to pixels.

In fig. 5.8(b) is presented the situation just after the lane change. The purple colored lines surrounding the central lane marking detail the search region for the lane marking. They signal that the lane marking equation uses a vertical formula $x = a * y + b$ due to the poor resolution of the normal equation $y = a * x + b$. The red bar at the bottom of fig. 5.8(b) shows the lateral displacement of the ego with respect to the middle of the lane (to the left).

The next figures will focus on object detection and tracking for each of the three different tracking models (lateral, regular and far).

In fig. 5.9(a) to fig. 5.9(d) is detailed the tracking of a lateral object from the very beginning until it transitions to the regular tracking model. The observed object is the silver Volkswagen Golf 4 Variant at the left of the image.

5.2 Results

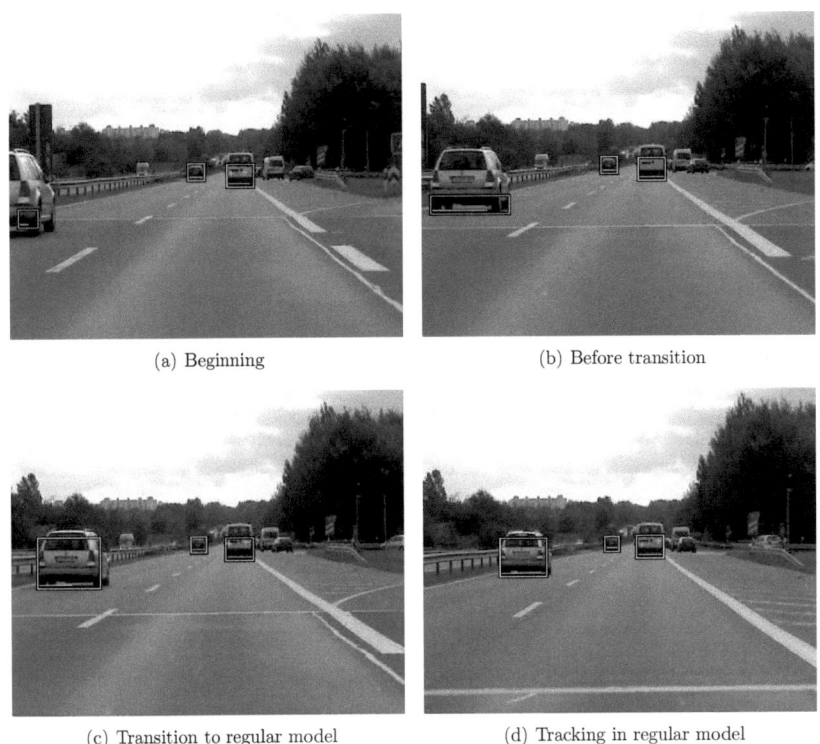

(a) Beginning   (b) Before transition

(c) Transition to regular model   (d) Tracking in regular model

Figure 5.9: Lateral object tracking and transition to regular object model in CCVS

The object enters the image from left - see fig. 5.9(a) - and stays in the lateral tracking model as long as it is less than 8 pixels distant from the left margin of the picture - see fig. 5.9(b) -. Note the robustness of the lateral object detection that is not influenced by the horizontal discontinuity in the street from fig. 5.9(b).

In fig. 5.9(c) the object has completely entered the picture and its tracking model switches to the regular tracking model. It will continue to be tracked in this model until it will be small enough to be handled by the far tracking model.

In fig. 5.10(a) to fig. 5.10(d) is presented the tracking of an object in the regular model. During the test we intentionally drove so that we covered lane change situations, intensity changes and curve driving all in the regular model. The position of the ego vehicle was between 30 to 80 meters behind the target vehicle. The sequence covers about 3 kilometres (about 1300 frames). The observed object is the dark green Volkswagen Golf 5 in the same lane as the ego vehicle.

129

Chapter 5

Figure 5.10: Regular object tracking in CCVS

The tracking begins in fact in fig. 5.8(a). Fig. 5.10(a) is just a few seconds after that lane change. The object is tracked without interruption due to the lateral cast shadows from the lateral vegetation (it was around 11 a.m. and the sun was at the right of camera) in 5.10(b).

There was another object entering - see fig. 5.10(c) - and exiting the scene (the blue Volkswagen Passat), but since it did not drive in the right lane, it did not overlap in the image with the object under observation.

The object is tracked without any problems until it begins to approach the left margin of the image, switches to the lateral model and then disappears from the image in the curve ahead. Fig. 5.10(d) is taken just before that.

The sequence selected for the illustration of the far object tracking is about 400 frames long. It shows a three lane highway (A2) and is taken during low traffic time. The visible objects are too far to be recognized; therefore they will be distinguished by their position

5.2 Results

(a) Frame 1 (b) Object lane change

(c) After overlapping (d) Frame 412

Figure 5.11: Far object tracking in CCVS

and estimated color, not by their type.

The sequence starts with two far objects that were detected and tracked in fig. 5.11(a). The silver car on the left maintains its lane, while the dark car on the right will perform a lane change ahead the silver one - see fig. 5.11(b) -. The dark object is accurately tracked during its lane change manoeuvre. It will be lost as it will overlap in the image with the silver vehicle - see fig. 5.11(c) -.

At the end of the sequence, another object was detected in the right lane in fig. 5.11(d). The detection is not perfect (two cars were detected as a single object) due to the very low resolution of the image in that point. Since the far object tracking model is based on form and does not analyse other aspects, the two cars will be identified together for a long time until the ego vehicle will come closer and they will be clearly distinguishable.

The fig. 5.17 sums up all the tracking principles. The sequence analyzed is about 450 frames, taken on the A39 highway, between the German cities Braunschweig and

Chapter 5

Wolfsburg, during the rush hour. The lighting is very strong, which reduces the color definition of the scene due to the camera adaptation. This situation is common in the automotive domain and raises no problems for the CCVS system.

The first frame (first row, left) presents two objects, both in the regular tracking model. The next frame (first row, right) shows the transition of the object in the left lane to the far tracking model and additionally illustrates the lateral tracking model.

Next (second row, left) the Volkswagen Golf 3 has changed to the lateral model. The next picture (second row, right) shows the transition of the Golf to the far model and the lost of the previously tracked object in that lane due to a lane change that makes it invisible (in front of the transporter in the ego lane).

The rest of the example pictures illustrate the quality of the object tracking. The scenes contain many cars, coming from left (entering the highway) or right (taking over the ego vehicle). The CCVS system works accurately, detecting and tracking even cars that are very hard to distinguish due to their partial overlapping with other vehicles.

5.2.3 Comparison with other vision systems

In order to be able to draw some conclusions about the advantages of the presented color vision system, two other systems were taken as a reference: a stereo greyscale system running on a dedicated high end machine (P4 3 GHz) and a mono greyscale system running on a relatively common configuration (PIII 1 GHz). Both systems were available at Volkswagen Group Research for tests and were integrated and tested in the same vehicle.

The analyzed sequence is 1800 seconds long. All three systems outputted their information on the CAN bus and the comparison was achieved by analysing the CAN log file.

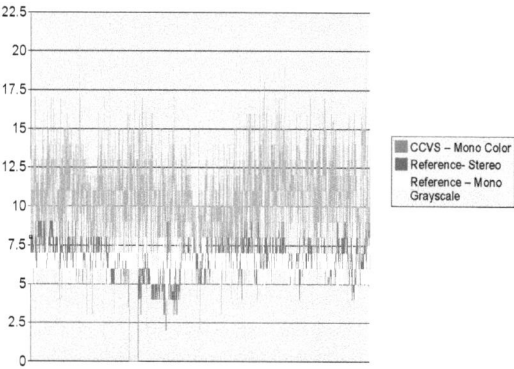

Figure 5.12: Framerate Comparision

5.2 Results

The graphic 5.12 lists the fps times over time for all three systems. The CCVS system slightly outpaces the stereo system and runs significantly faster than the greyscale mono system.

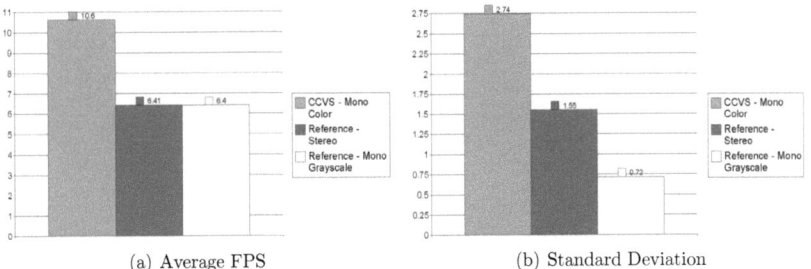

(a) Average FPS (b) Standard Deviation

Figure 5.13: Summary of the FPS Values

The summary in fig. 5.13(a) shows that the CCVS system is about 40% faster than the other two. The stereo system did not deliver lane information at all for 50 seconds between second 553 and 603. Therefore the average frame rate is just above the frame rate of the greyscale reference system.

One very interesting result is represented in 5.13(b) where the standard deviation of the measured frame rates is shown. The CCVS system has clearly the biggest deviation in the frame rate. One explanation is the absolute average value which is bigger. But the major source of these variations is the relative complex algorithm control methods in CCVS. The running time is proportional to the amount of the code that is executed and in CCVS this varies with the current driving situation and the number of detected objects.

The results are not very conclusive since the systems run on completely different computing architectures and at different CPU frequencies, but they support the conclusion that the current approach is able to sustain real time performance as defined by the other two systems (provided that CCVS runs on processors faster than 1,5 GHz).

The second test compares the results of the lane detection algorithms (car position in the lane). The reference is the stereo system which without doubt shows the best accuracy among all systems performing lane detection. It works with 3D models that include horizontal and vertical curvatures and is able to reconstruct 3D points from the scene to match to the model. The other two systems, greyscale mono and color mono, work with simple triangulation methods, which are less precise.

The fig. 5.14 shows the current lane width outputted on the CAN by the three systems. In order to be able to compare the data, for each system the output during a second was averaged and this average lane width value was used in our tests. The lane width is expressed in centimetres.

From fig. 5.14 it is clear that the stereo system is not only more accurate, but the

133

Chapter 5

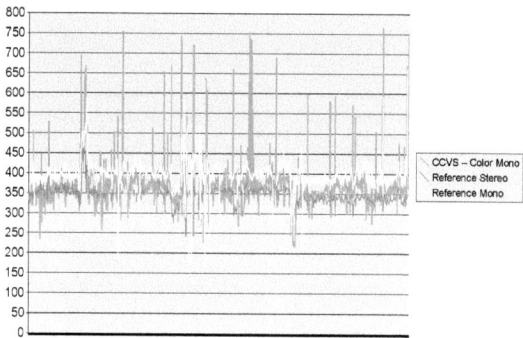

Figure 5.14: Comparison of the Lane Width Output

stability of its results over time is better. This is absolutely normal because it has the advantage of a much better way to reconstruct and track 3D information.

The CCVS system is the only system not employing any result tracking methods. Still, even a simple visual evaluation of the results shows that its output is closer to the reference stereo system than the output of the reference mono greyscale system. Considering also the fact that the CCVS system is optimized for the detection of far objects and therefore works with a larger focal lengths than the reference mono system (in the exemplified setup about 2 times larger), it is clear that the cognitive approach used to merge the results of more lane detection methods is delivering the expected results.

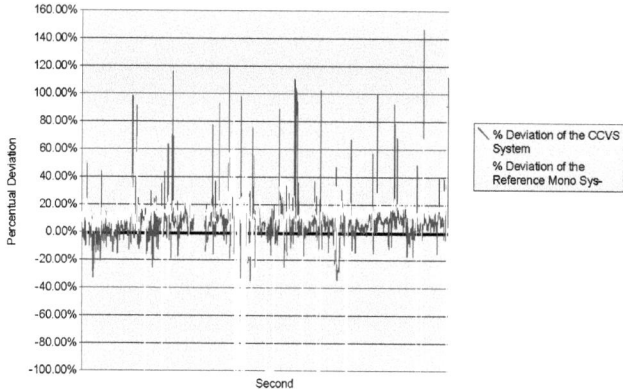

Figure 5.15: Deviation of the Lane Width Output

Fig. 5.15 illustrates the percentual deviation of the results from the output of the

5.2 Results

reference stereo system. The deviation of the CCVS system is about two times smaller than the deviation of the other mono system. This confirms the hypothesis that the methods used in CCVS deliver better results than the method used in the reference greyscale mono system. If the CCVS system uses tracking as well, then it could probably match the stereo system.

One observation is necessary regarding the data in fig. 5.15. Both mono systems may output lane widths twice the size of the real lane width when they detect the outer left and right markings, but not the one in the middle (for example, a lane change situation). This is not a problem because the association in the sensor fusion system handles more lane markings and is able to do the proper association. Therefore both mono systems were not tuned to eliminate this situation.

A direct comparison of the number of objects outputted by all three systems makes little or no sense since the reference stereo system also detects side delimiters, traffic signs, etc. On the contrary, the reference mono system uses a very simplified approach in which exclusively objects in the driving and neighbour lanes are detected. Therefore no direct comparison can take place.

Moreover, all three video systems use different lighting compensation methods specific to the underlying hardware. The reference stereo system has its own compensation algorithms with full control over the camera settings, while the CCVS system relies on the automatic compensation of the handycam. Comparing the object output in a single reference scene would also not yield reproducible results.

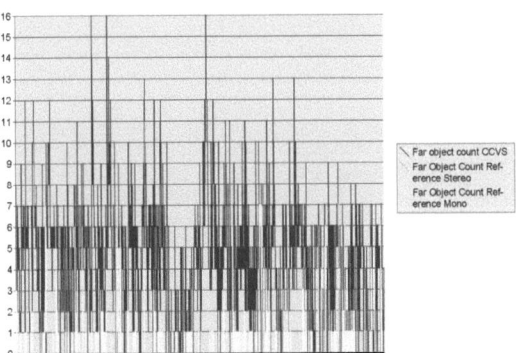

Figure 5.16: Number of detected objects beyond 100 meters

The graphic in fig. 5.16 shows the number of objects beyond the 100 meter limit (performance in the far range). In order for an object to be tracked continuously it has to have the same number of outputs as the numbers of frames in that time period. The sampling time was of 500 ms, which is for the CCVS system it should be 5-6 outputs for a single far object that is continuously tracked, for the reference mono or stereo 3-4 outputs. The results in fig. 5.16 show that:

135

Chapter 5

- the reference stereo system had a setup in which the objects beyond 100 meters were not outputted (for example in order to reduce the number of errors)
- the reference mono system is also unable to track objects in that range, the output consists mostly of isolated 3D reconstruction errors
- the only system that clearly shows that is able to track objects in the far range is the color mono system.

Figure 5.17: CCVS Object tracking - Putting it all together

Chapter 5

6 Conclusion & Future Work

6.1 Conclusion

6.1.1 Advantages over existing systems (color, monochrome)

This thesis presented a whole system as a standalone sensor using minimum of information from the car controller and the other systems present in the car. This makes the direct comparison of the results with other video systems as in 5.2.3 possible.

The most relevant results of this thesis are:

- higher frame rate than other systems due to improved software architecture. Separating the CAN communication, the GUI and the image display from the main processing thread allowed to drive them at different frame rates and eliminated all dead times. The CAN output was driven at the same frame rate as the processing, the GUI was updated on demand, the image display had an arbitrary rate (by default 8 fps).

This boosted the performance of the system. Along with the RGB to HSI conversion based on a lookup table with a 24 bit index it allowed the system to run in real time on hardware architectures based on processors faster than 1.5 GHz. This is not necessarily a great achievement, provided that real time greyscale video systems are encountered starting at few hundred Mhz. Such systems are mostly highly optimized algorithms implemented partially in assembly to make use of MMX or similar hardware acceleration techniques. In this software implementation, the much higher complexity of the approaches restricted the low level optimization possible to implement in the given timeframe.

- interpretation of the yellow markings in construction areas. Benefiting from the color information, this work deals actively and exclusively, for the first time in the field, with the recognizing of the yellow markings and their interpretation in the context (for example white markings that hold their significance are not eliminated from the result set). Moreover, the parameters of lane marking detection are adapted to improve the sensitivity of the detection in order to properly sense the smaller transitions in intensity characteristic to older and not so reflective yellow markings.

- extended range for object detection. The object detection in this work is a multiple model approach in which the complete visible spectrum is covered. While suffering from the common mono-camera weaknesses, the approach was extended to cover the complete range from 7-10 meters (closest visible object in the used camera setup) up to about 200-250 meters. This exceeds the capabilities of most vision systems developed for automotive applications. The extra gain in range is even more spectacular if considering that the object detection works with half of the standard PAL resolution (360 x 288 pixels).

Chapter 6

- simple and modular hardware structure. The system uses firewire and standard DirectX interfaces. This allows the use of virtually any digital camcorder with a DV output and of any laptop or computer that has a firewire input. There is no dedicated grabber, no need for additional video hardware. The requirements for the processor are average. The only expensive hardware part is the CAN interface to the car controller and the other driver assistance systems. Because cost is one of the most important issues in mass production environments, the simple and modular architecture along with the mass availability of the components is a key point for a driver assistance system.

6.1.2 What's New

Two new research areas were approached in this work. The first is related to processing algorithms working in the HSI color space. The other is the cognitive approach taken; non-mathematical representations (based on image structure and not on mathematical models) were used until the final step when the 3D information had to be generated for the output. The classical approach in automotive applications is to use a model that is extended and optimized until it covers the desired application area with good results. This is not only hard to do, but it is never possible to cover the complete range of environmental and illumination conditions with a single method. This work took another approach; it used several algorithms that have their strengths in different conditions and combined them to obtain superior results for a wider range of conditions.

Regarding the novel image processing methods this work introduced a method of segmenting the color images based on SI metrics. In slightly different forms, this method has already been mentioned in the existing literature. Still, until now it was not used in automotive applications. This work analyzed the HSI color space at great length and detailed the most important features that contribute to the success of this method. It analysed as well the particularities of the HSI space that generate unexpected effects. It has show how to compensate for these HSI space model problems, so that the final results of the color segmentation remain reliable.

Object detection was the area where color segmentation based on SI metrics was used most. Lane detection algorithms handle mostly greyscale information. Accordingly, the algorithms are based on monochromatic information. Still, lane detection in construction areas is hard to imagine without color information. This work presented the detection and filtering of yellow markings in detail.

Regarding the other new research aspect, the modelling of the environment without a strict mathematical model using multiple algorithms and merging their results, this work continues already existing methods in cognitive vision. Unfortunately, the timeframe of this work did not permit the in depth investigation of approaches based on neuronal networks or other forms of artificial intelligence. The implementation of the algorithms in this work is overwhelmingly based on knowledge of the environment and of the algorithms. Therefore most of the decisions regarding the weighting of the results of different algorithms are hard coded and not dynamically evaluated.

6.2 Future development

Looking back on the development of this vision system, it becomes obvious that during the research a lot of other possible promising development directions were ignored due to the lack of time, hardware and human resources.

The first area in which additional work may contribute to better performance is the color space used. The HSI space has model errors as shown in 3.2.1. These model errors could be eradicated by changing the lookup table used for the conversion. This would require first a very detailed analysis of all typical illumination situations and of the used algorithms. In lower illumination conditions, this may help providing much better saturation information.

The second main research direction to be continued should be the dynamical merging of subalgorithms and their control (enable, disable, change parameters) based on the recognition of on-going driving scene. This is a highly cognitive approach, very similar to the human focus on the interesting scene parts using already learnt methods to recognize objects. This may not only improve performance, but could also improve the quality of the final results by out-weighting the erroneous results, previous to the gathering of all partial results in the final output.

The third research direction that could bring real benefits to the system as a whole is the auto calibration of the system using the alternative calibration formulas from 4.5. Since by design the system is able to run without any calibration at all, the results could be interpreted and if they are not plausible, an auto calibration step should be performed.

Last, but not least, future research direction should focus on the integration of the sensor in more driver assistance systems. This is a key point to the success of the developed system in the long run.

Chapter 6

7 Notations and Definitions

Notation	Meaning	Definition and Remarks
BCB	Borland C++ Builder©	C++ Integrated Development Environment from Borland Software Corporation. http://www.borland.com
CAN	Controller Area Network	A serial bus device-level network for industrial automation. Addresses the needs of in-vehicle automotive communications
CCVS	Color Camera Vision System	The software system described in this Thesis.
DirectX	DirectX	A low-level API that provides user- mode media interfaces for games and other high-performance multimedia applications
GPU	Graphics Processing Unit	A single-chip processor located on the graphics card and used primarily for computing 3D functions. This includes things such as lighting effects, object transformations, and 3D motion
IDE	Integrated Development Environment	A complete programming environment containing at least an editor, compiler and linker in case of C++
IEEE1394a	FireWire Standard	A serial bus developed by Apple Computer and Texas Instruments (IEEE 1394 or FireWire). The High Performance Serial Bus can connect up to 63 devices in a tree-like daisy chain configuration, and transmit data at up to 400 megabits per second.It supports plug-and-play and peer-to-peer communication
INVENT	Intelligenter Verkehr und nutzergerechte Technik	
n/a	Not Available	There is no data or information for the position marked with "n/a"
OpenGL	Open Graphics Library	The premier environment for developing portable, interactive 2D and 3D graphics applications
RAD	Rapid Application Development	A system for quickly building application software. For example Microsoft Visual Basic©, Borland C++ Builder©, etc.
ROI	Region of Interest	Part of the image that is relevant for the processing algorithms.

143

Chapter 7

VCL	Visual Component Library	Borland Delphi© and C++ Builder© come with components that are part of a class hierarchy called the Visual Component Library (VCL). The VCL includes objects that are visible at runtime–such as edit controls, buttons, and other user-interface elements–as well as nonvisual controls like datasets and timers.
VCR	Videocassete Recorder	Also known as VTR for videotape recorder
Win32	Microsoft Windows 32 bit Platform	The programming platform that comprises of Windows 9x, Windows Milennium, Windows NT and later. Programs written for win32 will, with a few exceptions, run on all these systems
WinAPI	Windows Application Program Interface	the interface (calling conventions) application programs use for accessing services provided by some lower-level module (such as the operating system or JVM)

8 Appendix

8.1 Short description of included CD

The included CD contains the source code for the programs that are the subject of this work. Also on the CD is present the source of this document in form of LaTeXsource files. Also on the CD are present the LaTeXsource documents and PDFs of the articles that were published in relation with this PhD Thesis. Last, but not least is included a sequence of test images that cab be used for the test of the included programs. The structure is illustrated in 8.1.

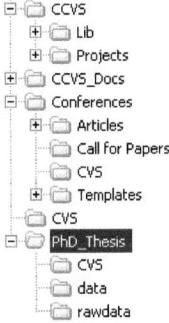

Figure 8.1: Directory layout of the included CD

The source code is stored under the CCVS directory. There are two subdirectories present at that level, called Lib and Projects. Under Lib are to be found all image processing, CAN interface, image acquisition and mathematical algorithms. These are shared between the programs that can be found in the Projects directory. The main programs that are part of the CCVS system were already described in 5.1.1.

The subdirectory Conferences stores the source and the final PDF versions of the articles that were published during the work that was performed for the PhD program. Each directory contains an article along with its raw source files. The list with the published articles is to be found in this directory in the file ArticleIndex.htm.

And last but not least the source files (text, images and data files) that were used to generate this work are stored in the PhD_Thesis subdirectory. Under the sub-subdirectory data are all files that were embedded in the final PDF document, while in raw data are the files that were used to generate them (e.g. the graphics in the document are to be found in data, while the excel tables or vectorial graphics used to generate them are in raw data).

8.2 Tools used to create this document

All names and marks that are mentioned in this work are copyrighted by their authors.

This document was created using the TeX Live freeware distribution of TeXthat can be found at http://www.tug.org/texlive/.

Image creation implemented frequently the Diagram Designer from http://logicnet.dk/meesoft/DiagramDesigner/.

9 Bibliography

[1] T. Aach and A. Kaup. Bayesian algorithms for adaptive change detection in image sequences using markov random fields. *Signal Processing: Image Communication* 7, pages 147–160, 1995.

[2] J. Badenas, J.M. Sanchiz, and F. Pla. Motion-based segmentation and region tracking in image sequences. *Pattern Recognition 34*, pages 661–670, 2001.

[3] M. Bertozzi and A. Broggi. Gold: A parallel real-time stereo vision system for generic obstacle and lane detection. *IEEE Transactions on Image Processing*, 7, 1998.

[4] M. Bertozzi, A. Broggi, and S. Castelluccio. A real-time oriented system for vehicle detection. *Journal of System Architecture*, pages 317–325, 1997.

[5] M. Betke, E. Haritaoglu, and L. S. Davis. Real-time multiple vehicle detection and tracking from a moving vehicle. *Machine Vision and Applications*, pages 69–83, 2000.

[6] S. Beucher and M. Bilodeau. Road segmentation and obstacle detection by a fast watershed transform. *Proceedings of IEEE Intelligent Vehicles*, page 296301, 1994.

[7] J.M. Blosseville, C. Krafft, F. Lenoir, V. Motyka, and S. Beucher. Titan: new traffic measurements by image processing. *Proceedings of IFAC Transportation systems, Tianjin*, 1994.

[8] Steven M. Boker. The representation of color metrics and mappings in perceptual color space. -, 1994.

[9] D. Brewster. On a new analysis of solar light. *Transactions of the Royal Society of Edinburgh*, 1831.

[10] C. Brodley and P. Utgoff. Multivariate decision trees. *Machine Learning*, 1995.

[11] A. Broggi. Parallel and local feature extraction: a real-time approach to road boundary detection. *IEEE Transaction on Image Processing 4*, 4:217223, 1995.

[12] A. Broggi and S. Berte. Vision-based road detection in automotive systems: a real-time expectation-driven approach. *Journal of Artificial Intelligence Research*, pages 325–348, 1995.

Bibliography

[13] T. Brown and J. Koplowitz. The weighted nearest neighbor rule for class dependent sample sizes. *IEEE Transactions on Information Theory*, page 617619, 1979.

[14] A.R. Bruss and B.K.P. Horn. Passive navigation. *Computer Vision, Graphics, and Image Processing 21*, pages 3–20, 1983.

[15] S.D. Buluswar and B.A. Draper. Color machine vision for autonomous vehicles. *Engineering Applications of Artificial Intelligence*, 1998.

[16] S. Carlsson and J.O. Eklundh. Object detection using model-based prediction and motion parallax. *Proceedings of Europe Conference on Computer Vision, Antibes*, pages 297–306, 1990.

[17] B. Coifman, D. Beymer, P. McLauchlan, and J. Malik. A real-time computer vision system for vehicle tracking and traffic surveillance. *Transportation Research Part C 6*, pages 271–288, 1998.

[18] D. Pomerlau D. and T. Jochem. Rapidly adapting machine vision for automated vehicle steering. *IEEE Expert*, 11:109–114, 1996.

[19] K.W. Dickinson and C.L. Wan. Road traffic monitoring using the trip ii system,. *IEEE Second International Conference on Road Traffic Monitoring*, pages 56–60, 1989.

[20] E.D. Dickmanns. Vehicle guidance by computer vision. *Concise Encyclopedia of Traffic and Transportation Systems*, 2004.

[21] E.D. Dickmanns and V. Graefe. Dynamic monocular machine vision. *Machine vision and applications 1*, pages 223–240, 1988.

[22] E.D. Dickmanns, B. Mysliwetz, and T. Christians. An integrated spatiotemporal approach to automatic visual guidance of autonomous vehicles. *IEEE Transactions on Systems, Man, and Cybernetics*, 20, 1990.

[23] E.D. Dickmanns and B.D. Mysliwetz. Recursive 3d road and relative ego-state recognition. *IEEE Pattern Analysis and Machine Intelligence*, 14:199213, 1992.

[24] L. Dreschler and H.-H. Nagel. Volumetric model and 3d-trajectory of a moving car derived from monocular tv-frame sequences of a street scene. *Computer Vision, Graphics, and Image Processing 20*, pages 199–228, 1982.

[25] M. Dubuisson and A. Jain. Contour extraction of moving objects in complex outdoor scenes. *International Journal of Computer Vision 14*, pages 83–105, 1995.

[26] W. Enkelmann. Investigations of multigrid algorithms for the estimation of optical flow fields in image sequences. *Computer Vision, Graphics, and Image Processing*, pages 150–177, 1988.

Bibliography

[27] W. Enkelmann. Interpretation of traffic scenes by evaluation of optical flow fields from image sequences. *IFAC Control Computers, Communications in Transportation*, 1989.

[28] W. Enkelmann. Obstacle detection by evaluation of optical flow field from image sequences. *Proceedings of European Conference on Computer Vision, Antibes*, 1990.

[29] W. Enkelmann, R. Kories, H.-H. Nagel, and G. Zimmermann. An experimental investigation of estimation approaches for optical flow fields. *Motion Understanding: Robot and Human Vision*, pages 189–226, 1987.

[30] W. Enkelmann, G. Struck, and J. Geisler. Roma - a system for modelbased analysis of road markings. *Proceedings of IEEE Intelligent Vehicles*, pages 356–360, 1995.

[31] M. Fathy and M.Y. Siyal. An image detection technique based on morphological edge detection and background differencing for realtime traffic analysis. *Pattern Recognition Letters 16*, pages 1321–1330, 1995.

[32] G.L. Foresti, V. Murino, and C. Regazzoni. Vehicle recognition and tracking from road image sequences. *IEEE Transactions on Vehicular Technology 48*, pages 301–317, 1999.

[33] G.L. Foresti, V. Murino, C.S. Regazzoni, and G. Vernazza. A distributed approach to 3d road scene recognition. *IEEE Transactions on Vehicular Technology 43*, 1994.

[34] R. Fraile and S.J. Maybank. Building 3d models of vehicles for computer vision. *Visual'99*, pages 697–702, 1999.

[35] G. Funka-Lea and R. Bajcsy. Combining color and geometry for the active, visual recognition of shadow. *Fifth International Conference on Computer Vision*, 1995.

[36] D. Geman and B. Jedynak. An active testing model for tracking roads in satellite images. *IEEE Pattern Analysis and Machine Intelligence*, 18:1–14, 1996.

[37] A. Giachetti, M. Campani, and V. Torre. The use of optical flow for road navigation. *IEEE Transactions on Robotics and Automation 14*, 1998.

[38] B. Gloyer, H.K. Aghajan, K.-Y. Siu, and T. Kailath. Video-based monitoring system using recursive vehicle tracking. *Proceedings of IS and T/SPIE Symposium on Electronic Image: Science and Technology- Image and Video Processing*, 1995.

[39] H. Grassmann. On the theory of compound colors. *Philosophical Magazine*, Serial 4:254–264, 1854.

[40] Allan Hanbury and Jean Serra. A 3d-polar coordinate colour representation suitable for image analysis. *Technical Report*, 2002.

Bibliography

[41] D.C. Hogg, G.D. Sullivan, K.D. Baker, and D.H. Mott. Recognition of vehicles in traffic scenes using geometric models. *IEEE Proceedings of the International Conference on Road Traffic Data Collection, London*, pages 115–119, 1984.

[42] N. Hoose. Computer image processing in traffic engineering. *Taunton Research Studies Press, UK*, 1991.

[43] N. Hoose. Impact: an image analysis tool for motorway analysis and surveillance. *Traffic Engineering Control Journal*, pages 140–147, 1992.

[44] N. Hoose. Computer vision as a traffic surveillance tool. *Proceedings of IFAC Transportation systems, Tianjin*, 1994.

[45] B.K.P. Horn and B.G. Schunck. Determining optical flow. *Artificial Intelligence 17*, pages 185–203, 1981.

[46] A.D. Houghton, G.S. Hobson, N.L. Seed, and R.C. Tozer. Automatic vehicle recognition. *IEEE Second International Conference on Road Traffic Monitoring*, pages 71–78, 1989.

[47] M. Irani and P. Anandan. A unified approach to moving object detection in 2d and 3d scenes. *IEEE Transactions on Pattern Analysis and Machine Intelligence 20*, pages 577–589, 1998.

[48] M. Irani, B. Rousso, and S. Peleg. Recovery of egomotion using region alignment. *IEEE Transactions on Pattern Analysis and MachineIntelligence 19*, pages 268–272, 1997.

[49] Badenas J., Bober M., and Pla F. Segmenting traffic scenes from grey level and motion information. *Pattern Analysis and Applications*, 4:28–38, 2001.

[50] R. Jain, R. Kasturi, and B. Schunck. Recovery of egomotion using region alignment. *Machine Vision, McGrawHill*, 1995.

[51] C. Jiangwei, J. Lisheng, G. L. Libibing, and W. Rongben. Study on method of detecting preceding vehicle based on monocular camera. *Proceedings of the Intelligent Vehicles Symposium*, 2004.

[52] C.R. Jung and C.R. Kelber. A lane departure warning system based on a linear-parabolic lane model. *Proceedings of the Intelligent Vehicles Symposium*, 2004.

[53] Y.-K. Jung and Y.-S. Ho. A feature-based vehicle tracking system in congested traffic video sequences. *PCM 2001*, pages 190–197, 2001.

[54] W. Kasprzak. An iconic classification scheme for video-based traffic sensor tasks. *CAIP*, page 725732, 2001.

Bibliography

[55] John R. Kender. Saturation, hue and normalised color: Calculation, digitization effects, and use. *Technical report, Department of Computer Science, Carnegie-Mellon University*, 2004.

[56] J.B. Kim, H.S. Park, M.H. Park, and H.J. Kim. A real-time region-based motion segmentation using adaptive thresholding and k-means clustering. *AI 2001*, pages 213–224, 2001.

[57] P. Klausmann, K. Kroschel, and D. Willersinn. Performance prediction of vehicle detection algorithms. *Pattern Recognition 32*, pages 2063–2065, 1999.

[58] K. Kluge and G. Johnson. Statistical characterization of the visual characteristics of painted lane markings. *Proceedings of IEEE Intelligent Vehicles*, pages 488–493, 1995.

[59] K. Kluge and S. Lakshmanan. A deformable-template approach to lane detection. *IEEE Proceedings of Intelligent Vehicles*, pages 54–59, 1995.

[60] D. Koller, K. Daniilidis, and H. Nagel. Model-based object tracking in monocular image sequences of road traffic scenes. *International Journal Computer Vision 10*, pages 257–281, 1993.

[61] R. Kories, H.-H. Nagel, and G. Zimmermann. Motion detection in image sequences: an evaluation of feature detectors. *Proceedings of International Joint Conference on Pattern Recognition, Montreal*, pages 778–780, 1984.

[62] R. Kories and G. Zimmermann. Workshop on motion: Representation and analysis. *IEEE Computer Society Press*, pages 101–106, 1986.

[63] C. Kreucher and S. Lakshmanan. Lana: a lane extraction algorithm that uses frequency domain features. *IEEE Transactions on Robotics and Automation*, 15, 1999.

[64] A. Kuehnel. Symmetry based recognition of the vehicle rears. *Pattern Recognition Letters 12*, pages 249–258, 1991.

[65] D.J. LeBlanc, G.E. Johnson, P.J.T. Venhovens, G. Gerber, R. DeSonia, R. Ervin, C.F. Lin, A.G. Ulsoy, and T.E. Pilutti. Capc: A roaddeparture prevention system. *IEEE Control Systems*, 1996.

[66] K.W. Lee, S.W. Ryu, S.J. Lee, and K.T. Park. Motion based object tracking with mobile. *Camera Electronics Letters 34*, pages 256–258, 1998.

[67] X. Li, Z.-Q. Liu, and K.-M. Leung. Detection of vehicles from traffic scenes using fuzzy integrals. *Pattern Recognition 35*, pages 967–980, 2002.

[68] A. Broggi M. Bertozzi. Vision-based vehicle guidance. *Computer Vision 30*, 1997.

Bibliography

[69] Luong Chi Mai. Introduction to computer vision and image processing. *Weblink: http://www.netnam.vn/unescocourse/computervision/computer.htm*, 2000.

[70] H.A. Mallot, H.H. Bulthoff, J.J. Little, and S. Bohrer. Inverse perspective mapping simplifies optical flow computation and obstacle detection. *Biological Cybernetics 64*, pages 177–185, 1991.

[71] S. Mantri and D. Bullock. Analysis of feedforward-backpropagation neural networks used in vehicle detection. *Transportation Research Part C 3*, pages 161–174, 1995.

[72] L. Matthies. Stereo vision for planetary rovers: stochastic modeling to near real-time implementation. *International Journal of Computer Vision 8*, pages 71–91, 1992.

[73] J.C. Maxwell. Experiments on colour, as perceived by the eye, with remarks on colour–blindness. *Transactions of the Royal Society of Edinburgh, 21*, pages 275–299, 1857.

[74] P.G. Michalopoulos and D.P. Panda. Derivation of advanced traffic parameters through video imaging. *IFAC Transportation Systems Chania, Greece*, 1997.

[75] H. Moon, R. Chellapa, and A. Rosenfeld. Performance analysis of a simple vehicle detection algorithm. *Image and Vision Computing 20*, pages 1–13, 2002.

[76] D.G. Morgenthaler, S.J. Hennessy, and D. DeMenthon. Range-video fusion and comparison of inverse perspective algorithms in static images. *IEEE Transactions on Systems Man and Cybernetics*, 20:13011312, 1990.

[77] A. Nagai, Y. Kuno, and Y. Shirai. Detection of moving objects against a changing background. *Systems and Computer in Japan 30*, pages 107–116, 1999.

[78] Makota Nagao, Takashi Matsuyama, and Yoshio Ikeda. Region extraction and shape analysis in aerial images. *Computer Graphics and Image Processing*, 10:195–223, 1979.

[79] H.-H. Nagel and W. Enkelmann. An investigation of smoothness constrains for the estimation of displacement vector fields from image sequences. *IEEE Transactions on Pattern Analysis and Machine Intelligence*, pages 565–593, 1986.

[80] H.H. Nagel. Constraints for the estimation of displacement vector fields from image sequences. *Proceedings of Intelligent Joint Conference on Artificial Intelligence*, pages 945–951, 1983.

[81] S. Nedevschi, R. Schmidt, Th. Graf, and et al. R. Danescu. 3d lane detection system based on stereovision. *IEEE Conference on Intelligent Transportation Systems*, 2004.

[82] A.Y. Nooralahiyan and H.R. Kirby. Vehicle classification by acoustic signature. *Mathematical and Computer Modeling*, 27:911, 1998.

[83] M. Papageorgiou. Video sensors. *Concise Encyclopedia of traffic and transportation systems*, pages 610–615, 1991.

[84] N. Paragios and R. Deriche. Geodesic active contours and level sets for the detection and tracking of moving objects. *IEEE Transactions on Pattern Analysis and Machine Intelligence 22*, pages 266–280, 2000.

[85] N. Paragios and G. Tziritas. Adaptive detection and localization of moving objects in image sequences. *Signal Processing: Image Communication 14*, pages 277–296, 1999.

[86] Y. Park. Shape-resolving local thresholding for object detection. *Pattern Recognition Letters 22*, pages 883–890, 2001.

[87] R.C.Gonzalez and R.E. Woods. Digital image processing. *ISBN 0130946508*, 1993.

[88] C. Rotaru, Th. Graf, and J. Zhang. Extracting road features from color images using a cognitive approach. *Proceedings of Intelligent Vehicles Symposium, Parma, Italy*, 2004.

[89] C. Rotaru, Th. Graf, and J. Zhang. Special cases of lane detection in construction areas. *Advanced Microsystems for Automotive Applications*, 2005.

[90] J. Schick and E.D. Dickmanns. Simultaneous estimation of 3d shape and motion of objects by computer vision. *Proceedings of IEEE Workshop on Visual Motion, Princeton, NJ*, pages 256–261, 1991.

[91] K. Shimizu and N. Shigehara. Image processing system used cameras for vehicle surveillance. *IEEE Second International Conference on Road Traffic Monitoring*, pages 61–65, 1989.

[92] E. Silk. Human detection and recognition for an hors doeuvres serving robot. *Data structures and network algorithms*, 1983.

[93] S.M. Smith and J.M. Brady. A scene segmenter; visual tracking of moving vehicles. *Engineering Applications of Artificial Intelligence 7*, pages 191–204, 1994.

[94] A. Soto, M. Saptharishi, A. Trebi Ollennu, J. Dolan, and P. Khosla. Cyber-atvs: Dynamic and distributed reconnaissance and surveillance using all terrain ugv. *Proceedings of the International Conference on Field and Service Robotics*, pages 329–334, 1999.

[95] G.D. Sullivan, K.D. Baker, A.D. Worrall, C.I. Attwood, and P.M. Remagnino. Model-based vehicle detection and classification using orthographic approximations. *Image and Vision Computing 15*, pages 649–654, 1997.

Bibliography

[96] T.N. Tan, G.D. Sullivan, and K.D. Baker. Model-based location and recognition of road vehicles. *International Journal of Computer Vision 27*, pages 5–25, 1998.

[97] C.J. Taylor, J. Malik, and J. Weber. A real time approach to stereopsis and lane-finding. *IFAC Transportation Systems Chania, Greece*, 1997.

[98] A. Techmer. Real-time motion based vehicle segmentation in traffic lanes. *DAGM 2001*, pages 202–207, 2001.

[99] T. ten Kate, R. van Leeuwen, B. Driessen, E. Wilmink, and F. Groen. Passing vehicle detection with a mobile camera. *10th World Congress on ITS, Spain*, 2004.

[100] F. Thomanek, E.D. Dickmanns, and D. Dickmanns. Multiple object recognition and scene interpretation for autonomous road vehicle guidance. *Proceedings of IEEE Intelligent Vehicles*, pages 231–236, 1994.

[101] C. Thorpe, M. Hebert, T. Kanade, and S. Shafer. Vision and navigation for the carnegie-mellon navlab. *IEEE Transactions on Pattern Analysis and Machine Intelligence*, 10:362–373, 1988.

[102] E. Trucco and A. Verri. Introductory techniques for 3-d computer vision. *ISBN 0-13-261108-2 Prentice Hall International*, pages 15–50, 179–180, 1998.

[103] S. Tsugawa. Vision-based vehicles in japan: machine vision systems and driving control systems. *IEEE Transactions on Industrial Electronics 41 (4)*, pages 398–405, 1994.

[104] M.A. Turk, D.G. Morgenthaler, K.D. Gremban, and M. Marra. Vits - a vision system for autonomous land vehicle navigation. *IEEE Transactions on Pattern Analysis and Machine Intelligence*, 10, 1998.

[105] Kastrinaki V., Zervakis M., and Kalaitzakis K. A survey of video processing techniques for traffic applications. *Image and Vision Computing*, 21:359–381, 2003.

[106] S.A. Velastin, J.H. Yin, M.A. Vicencio-Silva, A.C. Davies, R.E. Allsop, and A. Penn. Image processing for on-line analysis of crowds in public areas. *Proceedings of IFAC Transportation systems, Tianjin*, 1994.

[107] H. von Helmholtz. On the theory of compound colours. *Philosophical Magazine*, Serial 4:519–535, 1852.

[108] C.L. Wan and K.W. Dickinson. Road traffic monitoring using image processing-a survey of systems, techniques and applications. *IFAC Control Computers, Communications in Transportation*, 1989.

[109] C.L. Wan, K.W. Dickinson, and T.D. Binnie. A cost-effective image sensor system for transport applications utilising a miniature cmos single chip camera. *Proceedings of IFAC Transportation systems, Tianjins*, 1994.

Bibliography

[110] Chengye Wang, Liuqing Hunag, and Azriel Rosenfeld. Detecting clouds and cloud shadows on aerial photograps. *Pattern Recognition Letters*, 12:55–64, 1991.

[111] Y. Wang, D. Shen, and E.K. Teoh. Lane detection using spline model. *Pattern Recognition Letters*, pages 677–689, 1994.

[112] J. Weber, D. Koller, Q.-T. Luong, and J. Malik. An integrated stereobased approach to automatic vehicle guidance. *Proceedings of the Fifth ICCV*, pages 12–20, 1995.

[113] J. Weber, D. Koller, Q.-T. Luong, and J. Malik. New results in stereobased automatic vehicle guidance. *Proceedings of IEEE Intelligent Vehicles*, pages 530–535, 1995.

[114] C. Wohler and J.K. Anlauf. Real-time object recognition on image sequences with the adaptable time delay neural network algorithm - applications for autonomous vehicles. *Image and Vision Computing 19*, pages 593–618, 2001.

[115] Y. Won, J. Nam, and B.-H. Lee. Image pattern recognition in natural environment using morphological feature extraction. *Proceedings of the Joint IAPR International Workshops on Advances in Pattern Recognition*, pages 806–815, 2001.

[116] T. Young. On the theory of light and colors. *Philosophical Transactions of the Royal Society*, 91:12–49, 1802.

[117] X. Yu, S. Beucher, and M. Bilodeu. Road tracking, lane segmentation and obstacle recognition by mathematical morphology. *Proceedings of IEEE Intelligent Vehicle*, page 166170, 1992.

[118] A.L. Yuille and J.M. Coughlan. Fundamental limits of bayesian inference: order parameters and phase transitions for road tracking. *IEEE Pattern Analysis and Machine Intelligence*, pages 160–173, 2000.

[119] J. Zhang and H. Nagel. Texture-based segmentation of road images. *IEEE Intelligent Vehicles*, 1994.

Bibliography

List of Figures

1.1	The Future of the Driver Assistance Systems	7
3.1	Theoretical HSI Space and RGB Spaces	41
3.2	HSI Space Obtained from 24 Bit RGB	42
3.3	Sample Image and its H, S, I components	43
3.4	Histograms of the I, S Values of Image Points	44
3.5	Saturation-Intensity Histogram of the Scene	46
3.6	Correspondence between the SI histogram and the original image	46
3.7	Example of SI footprint of small chromatic objects	47
3.8	Example of SI footprint of large chromatic objects	47
3.9	Overimposed Results using the Weighting Function F_3	50
3.10	Normal 3 lane highway scene	51
3.11	Low contrast, concrete surface	52
3.12	High contrast scene, close car	53
3.13	Saturated image	54
3.14	Fog scene	54
3.15	Free highway, with traffic shield	55
3.16	Bright image, almost saturated	58
3.17	Bright image, lateral shadow	58
3.18	Bright image, with shadows	59
3.19	Normal brightness	59
3.20	Normal brightness with close object	60
3.21	Reduced brightness	60
3.22	Low brightness image	61
3.23	Low brightness image, truck	61
3.24	Underexposed image	62
3.25	Comparison with other segmentation algorithms - low contrast scene . .	64
3.26	Detail comparison - low contrast scene	64
3.27	Comparison with other segmentation algorithms - close scene	65
3.28	Comparison with other segmentation algorithms - far objects	65
3.29	Comparison with other segmentation algorithms - different objects . . .	65
3.30	CCVS Algorithms - Top-level Structure	67
3.31	CCVS-Online - Threaded Structure	70
3.32	Diagram of the system	73

List of Figures

3.33	Road and lane markings sampling areas	73
3.34	Road and lane markings detection: Vertical Fill Algorithm	74
3.35	Road pre-detection and lane markings detection	76
3.36	Road and lane marking detection	77
3.37	Regions of Interests for SI Metric Computation	79
3.38	Results of applying the SI Metric to the ROIs	81
3.39	Lane Boundary Detection based on Road Predetection Results	83
3.40	Color Features of the Yellow Markings	84
3.41	Typical yellow markings in construction areas	86
3.42	Yellow Marking Detection Algorithm	88
3.43	Structure of the Lane Interpreter	89
3.44	Scene with three different car models (Far, Regular, Lateral)	93
3.45	Object Detection and Tracking	94
3.46	Candidate Object Detection	95
3.47	SI Metric Results for Object Detection	96
3.48	Object Detection Results using the SI Metric	97
3.49	Object Detection Results using the Road Detection Results	98
3.50	Lateral Object Detection and Tracking Results	99
3.51	Far Object Detection	100
3.52	SI Metric for Object Alignment of the Newly Detected Objects	103
3.53	Transition to Specific Tracking Model	104
3.54	Tracking the positioning for regular objects	105
3.55	Handling shadows during the tracking of regular objects	106
3.56	Tracking backlights to assist regular object tracking	107
3.57	Software Diagram for Far Object Tracking	109
3.58	Correlation Areas	109
3.59	Detection Templates and Corresponding Samples	110
3.60	Object tracking example	111
4.1	Estimating the ego lateral position	116
4.2	Depth estimation using object baseline	117
4.3	Depth estimation using object width	118
4.4	Errors in Depth reconstruction	120
5.1	CCVS-Dev - GUI Interface	123
5.2	CCVS-Online - Basic Application Structure	124
5.3	Basic Hardware Diagram	125
5.4	Image Acquisition and Processing - Hardware Options	125
5.5	In-Car Deployment Of Vision Sensors	126
5.6	Sensors - deployment and range	126
5.7	Interconnection Network over CAN	127
5.8	Handling of a lane change situation	128
5.9	Lateral object tracking and transition to regular object model in CCVS	129
5.10	Regular object tracking in CCVS	130

5.11	Far object tracking in CCVS	131
5.12	Framerate Comparision	132
5.13	Summary of the FPS Values	133
5.14	Comparison of the Lane Width Output	134
5.15	Deviation of the Lane Width Output	134
5.16	Number of detected objects beyond 100 meters	135
5.17	CCVS Object tracking - Putting it all together	137
8.1	Directory layout of the included CD	145

Die VDM Verlagsservicegesellschaft sucht für wissenschaftliche Verlage abgeschlossene und herausragende

Dissertationen, Habilitationen, Diplomarbeiten, Master Theses, Magisterarbeiten usw.

für die kostenlose Publikation als Fachbuch.

Sie verfügen über eine Arbeit, die hohen inhaltlichen und formalen Ansprüchen genügt, und haben Interesse an einer honorarvergüteten Publikation?

Dann senden Sie bitte erste Informationen über sich und Ihre Arbeit per Email an *info@vdm-vsg.de*.

Sie erhalten kurzfristig unser Feedback!

VDM Verlagsservicegesellschaft mbH
Dudweiler Landstr. 99
D - 66123 Saarbrücken
www.vdm-vsg.de

Telefon +49 681 3720 174
Fax   +49 681 3720 1749

Die VDM Verlagsservicegesellschaft mbH vertritt

Printed by Books on Demand GmbH, Norderstedt / Germany